The Brush Dances

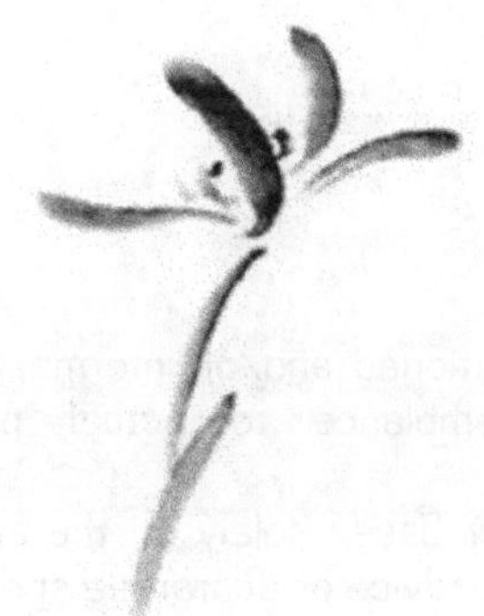

Roslyn Levin, SCA

ISBN 978-1-9993936-0-1

For information: www.artbyroslyn.on.ca

First edition
Published and printed in Canada

People, places or incidents mentioned and/or information provided herein reflect solely the author's viewpoint. Any resemblance to actual persons, living or dead, business establishments, events, or
locales is entirely coincidental or based solely on the author's perspective. This book is not intended to provide personalized advice or guarantee specific results, as results are dependent upon many individual factors which are beyond control of the author.

This book was written, edited and published by the author. Work is included as provided by the author, views expressed are those of the author and any errors, omissions or otherwise are the author's responsibility.

Acknowledgements

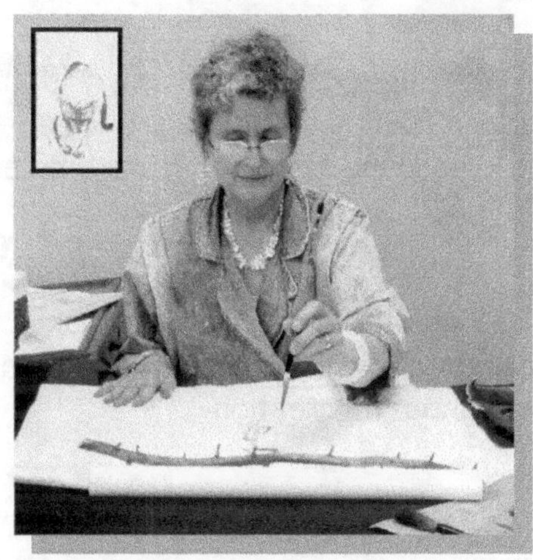

This book would not have been possible without the help of so many people.
I would like to first thank my two sensei, Tomoko Kodama and Noriko Maeda, to whom this book is dedicated.

It would not have been possible for me to properly formulate all the ideas presented in this book without the teachings of my many students, who have filled my life with challenges and joy.

Joan Hope, who owns and operates Dragonfly Arts on Broadway, which has housed my studio for more than 10 years, has encouraged me in all my artistic endeavours.

Thanks also go to my friend and fellow artist, Jennifer McKinnon (www.turnoffatestudio.ca), who is a woodturner extraordinaire. She courageously offered to try and paint using the instructions herein!

I would also like to acknowledge the work of my publishing team at TRIMATRIX Management Consulting Inc., who have lead me through the maze of creating an actual book!

Andrew Cherry, my husband, who supports me, not only with his love and encouragement, but also by making stretchers and frames for all my art. He ensures that I eat on a regular schedule when I am in full workaholic mode, and is more than any artist could hope for in a life partner.

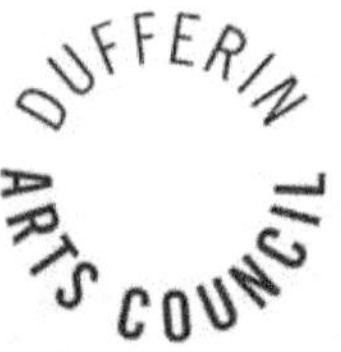

I also wish to thank the Dufferin Arts Council for awarding me the Reed T. Cooper Bursary, enabling me to produce this book, and also for their patience throughout its creation.

Dedication

I was introduced to sumi-e by **Tomoko Kodama** in 1976 at the Ottawa School of Art. Over the years she became my sensei (teacher), my mentor and my friend. She not only taught many students to paint in sumi-e, but she also developed the Body, Breath, Brush method of painting in Oriental brushstroke technique, and formed Group Yohaku (White Space), through which many Canadian sumi-e artists were able to show work in both China and Japan.

Tomoko's untimely death in 2010 was a great blow to all who knew and cared for her.

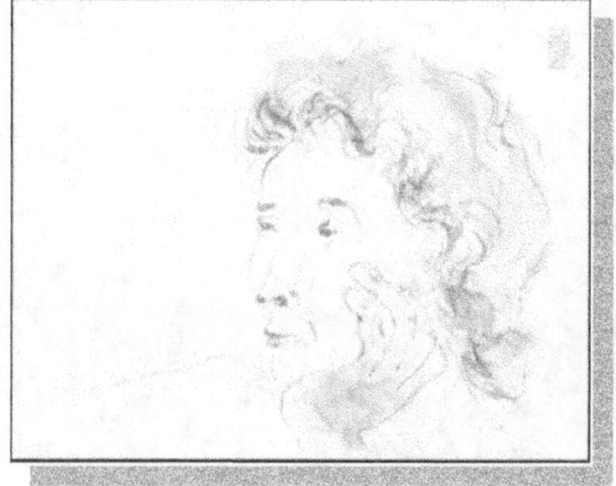

Portrait of Tomoko Kodama by author

A haiku for Tomoko

Her brush is stilled here on earth
but her ink sings always
oh, such beautiful clouds

Noriko Maeda, my shodo (Japanese calligraphy) instructor, shares the dedication of this book with Tomoko.

I searched for more than 20 years for a sensei who could help me grow further as a sumi-e artist. Until I met Noriko Maeda, I had not found such a person. Noriko-sensei continually challenges me to improve my brushstrokes and composition. She has also helped me with understanding the Japanese culture.

Noriko-sensei is responsible for working with me to choose my Japanese artist name, "Shun Swee" ("Spring Water"), which is a reflection of who I am and how I paint. Noriko-sensei has also taught me the art of tenkoku (stamp carving) through her day-long classes each summer. I so enjoy this part of sumi-e that I have carved more than 30 hanko (namestamps) with various meanings in Japanese.

Noriko instigated the formation of Shodo Canada in 2008, through which I have participated along with all her students, and others throughout Canada, in having our calligraphy juried annually by Japanese Master calligraphers in Japan. They are then returned to Canada on traditional scrolls for display at the Japanese Canadian Cultural Centre in Toronto.

Testimonial

Roslyn Levin has been a dedicated, constantly-evolving sumi-e student, artist and teacher during the more than 20 years I have known her through The Japanese Paper Place. Her continual openness to every aspect of the art form, including to many variations of washi, has resulted in a brilliant intuitive style, which appears deceptively spontaneous. Her works are marked by forceful gentleness and grace, which continues to be readily recognized by her appreciative clientele.

Her ongoing fresh approach to materials, technique and subject matter after so many years of study and practice are indicative of the wisdom she exemplifies in the Zen concept shoshin — "always a beginner's mind."

Her many students have been moved, delighted and improved immeasurably by her clarity of instruction, her organization and her warmth and humour. What a gift she, and her new book, are to the too-little known world of sumi-e painting!

Nancy Jacobi
President
The Japanese Paper Place
www.japanesepaperplace.com

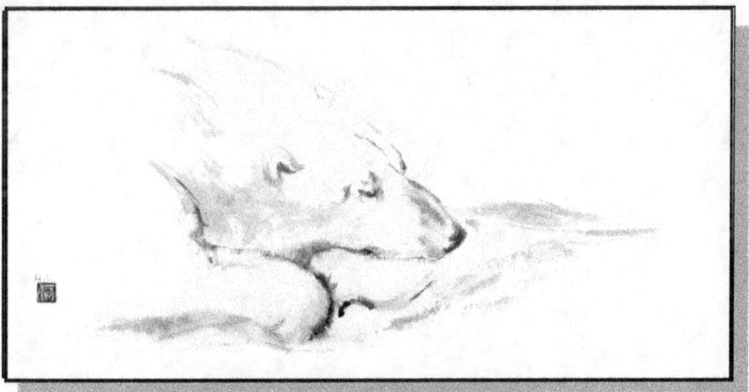

Ice Bear Dreams by author
Hanko is "Spring Water" - author's artist name

Contents

Introduction i

History 1

The Method and Personal Thoughts on Sumi-e....................... 3

Arrangement of the Work Area 6

Sumi – Black Ink 7

Suzuri – Inkstone 8

Fude – The Brush 9

Washi – Japanese Paper 12

Felt 14

Preparing the Ink 15

Hanko or Name Stamps 17

How to Hold and Wet Your Brush 19

Your First Brushstrokes.................. 21

Crocus 30

Bamboo 40

Pear 51

Wild Orchid.................. 59

Chrysanthemum 71

Plum Blossom.................. 79

How to Stretch and Wet-Mount a Sumi-e Painting................ 91

About the Author.................. 97

Introduction

Sumi-e, the ancient form of Japanese painting, can be mastered using only four simple tools:

- Sumi (ink)
- Suzuri (inkstone)
- Fude (brush)
- Washi (paper)

The artist depicts the essence of what he/she is trying to portray with as few brushstrokes as possible — simply and elegantly, but with strength in each line or shade.

Sumi-e is a mindfulness meditation. It is a metaphor for our journey through life. It is a way to grow spiritually, one brushstroke at a time.

This is my chosen medium and who I am.

Sumi-e, for me, is my ikigai — my reason for being!

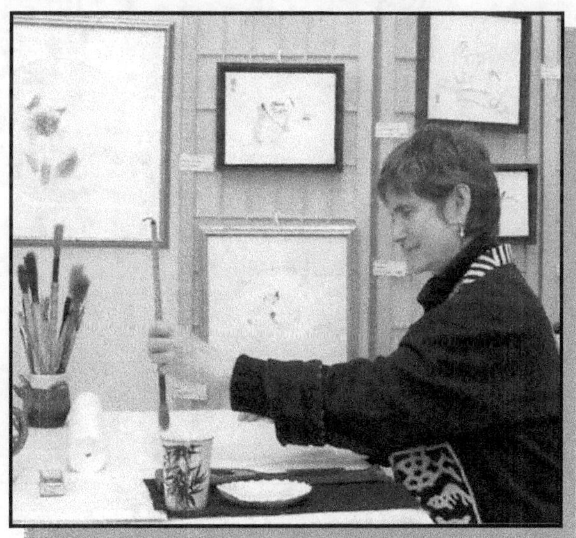

History

Oriental brushstroke is an art form thousands of years old. Its history parallels that of Buddhism.

The Buddhist monks would use brushstroke painting to aid them in their meditation practice. As Buddhism moved across the Orient, so did brushstroke painting. Each country put its own cultural stamp upon the technique. Although the same brush strokes were — and still are — always used, in some countries the technique became more colourful and ornamental, and in others it became more of a discipline.

In Japan, this art form became a very Zen moving meditation, bringing the paintings down to the fewest number of brushstrokes needed to portray what is in the artist's soul.

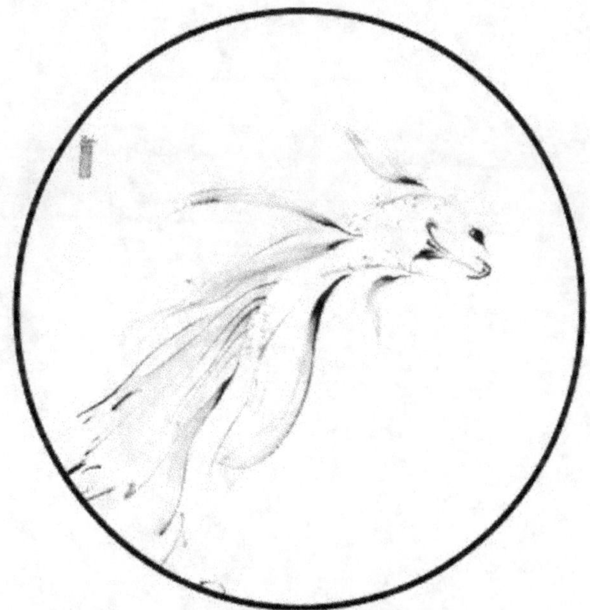

Water Dance by author
Hanko is "Roslyn" in Japanese phonetics

The Method and Personal Thoughts on Sumi-e

In this series of lessons, you will learn to paint in a minimalist form, using as few brushstrokes as possible to create your image in black and varying shades of gray. Each image will capture the essence of what you are trying to portray.

Colour may be added as well, if the artist wishes, but it is not necessary for the success of the finished piece. I have not included colour in the pieces shown in this book, although I do occasionally use watercolour, usually sparingly, in my work.

The technique described builds upon the work of Tomoko Kodama, my sensei, who developed the 3 Bs (Body, Breath, Brush) method, with the help of her students during her more than 40 years of teaching brushstroke painting in Ottawa, Ontario, Canada.

This technique uses the brush as an extension of the spirit and body of the artist, and incorporates movement and breathing to create brushstrokes of great strength.

In sumi-e, you are attempting to paint your subject in the simplest manner possible.

There is a sense of space in Japanese paintings that is not usually present in other forms of visual art. What is left to the viewer's imagination is at least as important as what is seen.

There are feelings of energy and peace in these paintings.

Balance is actualized by the presence of areas of white space (yohaku), creating what can only be described as Zen.

Texture is achieved through the wetness of the brush or paper, which can become wet as you paint, and the speed with which the brush is used.

Different textures will also be achieved depending upon whether the rough (unsized) or smooth (sized) side of the paper is used.

Before each brushstroke is applied, the artist must ask: "Is this brushstroke necessary?"

If it is applied and the artist realizes it did not add to the whole, or if there is something not quite right about it in the artist's opinion, the painting is begun again.

One asks not only, "How does it look?" but also, "How does it feel?"

One is certainly in the realm of spirit here.

So let the Adventure begin!

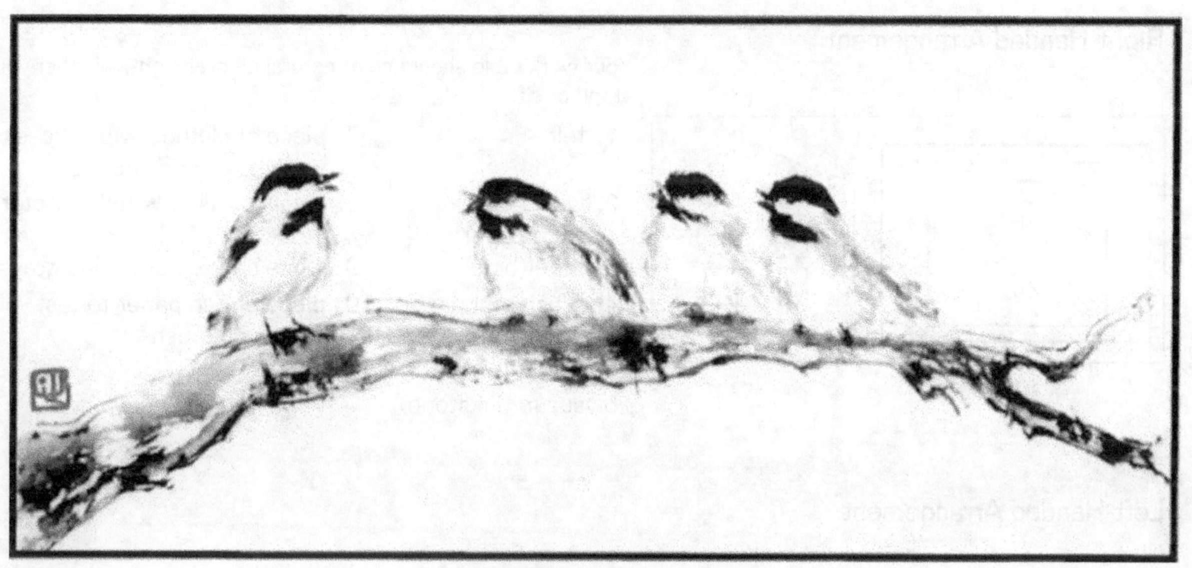

Choir Practice by the author
Hanko is "Heart/Mind/Spirit"

Arrangement of the Work Area

In sumi-e, the neatness of the artist's space is a reflection of the clarity within their mind and heart, allowing the creative spirit to flow.

Right-Handed Arrangement

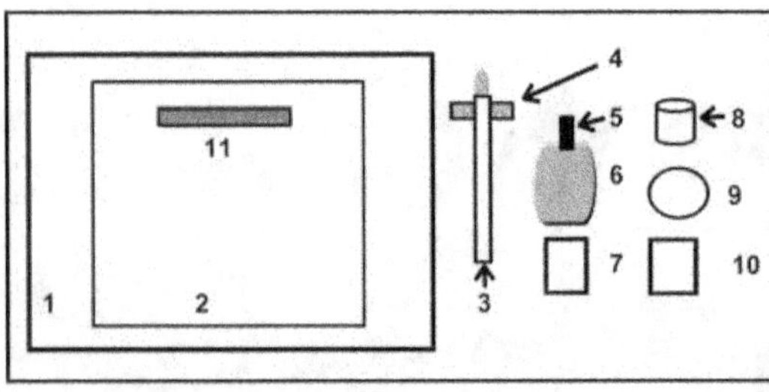

Your work table should be at natural elbow height, whether you stand or sit.

1. felt
2. washi (rice paper)
3. fude (brush)
4. brush rest
5. sumi (inkstick)
6. suzuri (inkstone)
7. piece of cloth to wipe excess water or ink off the brush
8. small jar filled ¼ full of water
9. white saucer for mixing grays
10. piece of rice paper to test colour on brush
11. paperweight

Left-Handed Arrangement

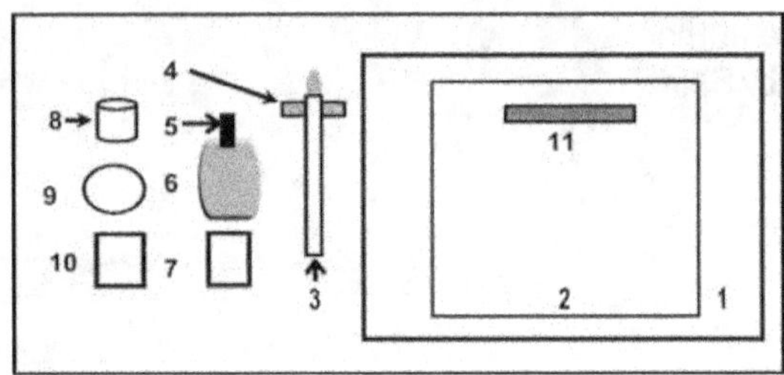

Note: The inkstone & inkstick may be replaced with liquid ink on a flat dish, but this will not give you the same tones & variations of grays.

*The hand that does not use the brush will rest gently on the felt.

Sumi – Black Ink

Sumi, the black ink used in brushstroke painting, is made from pine or vegetable soot.

The ink is unlike India Ink or bottled ink. It has a translucency, transparency and vibrancy.

It can be true black, blue-black or brown-black. In Japan, the blue-black is the most prized.

You cannot necessarily tell the quality of the ink by the price, but it is usually a good indicator. Many inksticks have a coating to protect them that prevents the artist from achieving a rich black colour. If your new inkstick appears to produce at most a dark gray, when it is dry, sand the end with a bit of fine wet/dry sandpaper to remove the coating.

Older inksticks are said to age like wine and become even better over time.

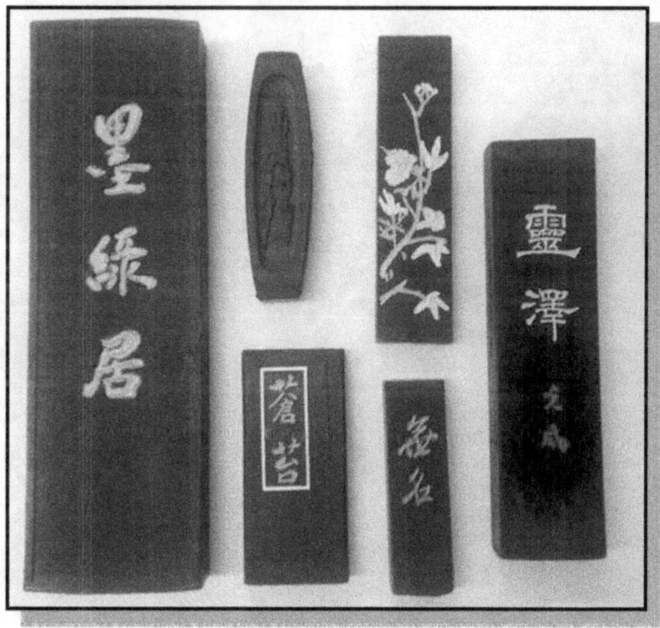

Suzuri – Inkstone

The inkstone typically has a well area to hold the water, and a flat area for grinding the ink, although you will find many inkstones without the well area.

Inkstones can be made of a variety of materials, from slate to metal and jade. There are specific geographical locations in both China and Japan that have stone that is used to produce wonderful, naturally coloured and/or shaped suzuri. What all suzuri share in common is a flat surface with microscopic grooves to allow for the smooth grinding of ink.

Some of the most beautiful suzuri have very natural-looking shapes or colours. The original roughness of the stone may be preserved along the edge, or a carved bas-relief may be used as decoration.

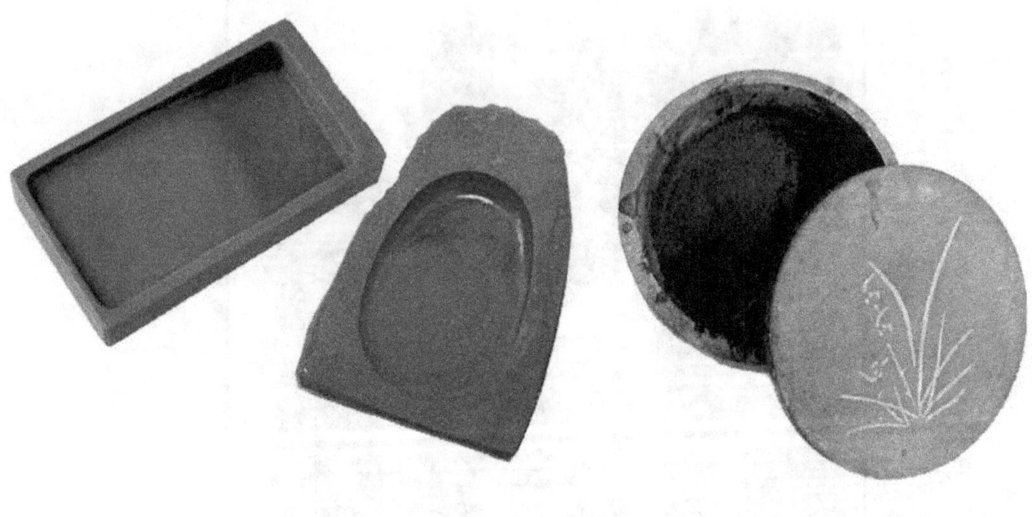

Fude – The Brush

The handle on most oriental brushes is made of bamboo, but it can be made from any wood as well as metal, ivory or even jade.

Take care not to wet the handle, because some materials can crack, or the glue holding the brush to the handle can be damaged. Definitely do not leave it soaking in water as you perform other tasks.

Commonly, the hair of sumi-e brushes can be goat, sheep, horse, wolf, or ox. Any hair that has never been cut can be used for this purpose, as uncut hair has a soft, rounded end.

Oriental brushes are not made in the same manner as Western brushes. The inner hairs of a typical Oriental brush are short. As the layers of hairs are added, they become longer and longer, allowing every brush, no matter how large at the base, to have a very sensitive point that can draw the finest line.

I have made brushes using goat, deer, lynx, raccoon, badger, bear and skunk hair, as well as feathers.

Each brush is an adventure in painting, as no two brushes will react the same way in the hand of the artist.

How to treat a New Brush

When you have a new brush, it will often be hardened with a starch. Gently bend the brush back and forth to soften the hairs, beginning at the tip and working your way down the brush. Gently wash the brush in water — never hot water, and never with soap — by dipping it in the water and then squeezing out the water between your thumb and first finger over and over until the water runs clear and the brush is wet throughout.

When I began to paint in sumi-e, I had a rather small and very inexpensive brush.

A few weeks after I began, Madame Kodama was selling some lovely brushes to many of the students in the class.

When I expressed interest in a new and better brush, she would not allow it. She said that I was very good, and if I could paint with the brush I had, I would be able to paint with any brush.

At the time I was disappointed, but she was, of course, correct.

I am now both an avid brush collector and a brush maker.

Take care to only soften the bottom half of the hairs. This is especially important for beginners, as it allows for better brush control.

I prefer a brush about ¼" wide at the base and 1.5" to 2" in length; however, any brush is a good brush once you learn how to use it!

For beginners, if the hairs are too soft or too long for good control, wind a length of cotton thread tightly around the base, near the handle, and tie it off so that it will not distract you while painting. The thread can be removed later.

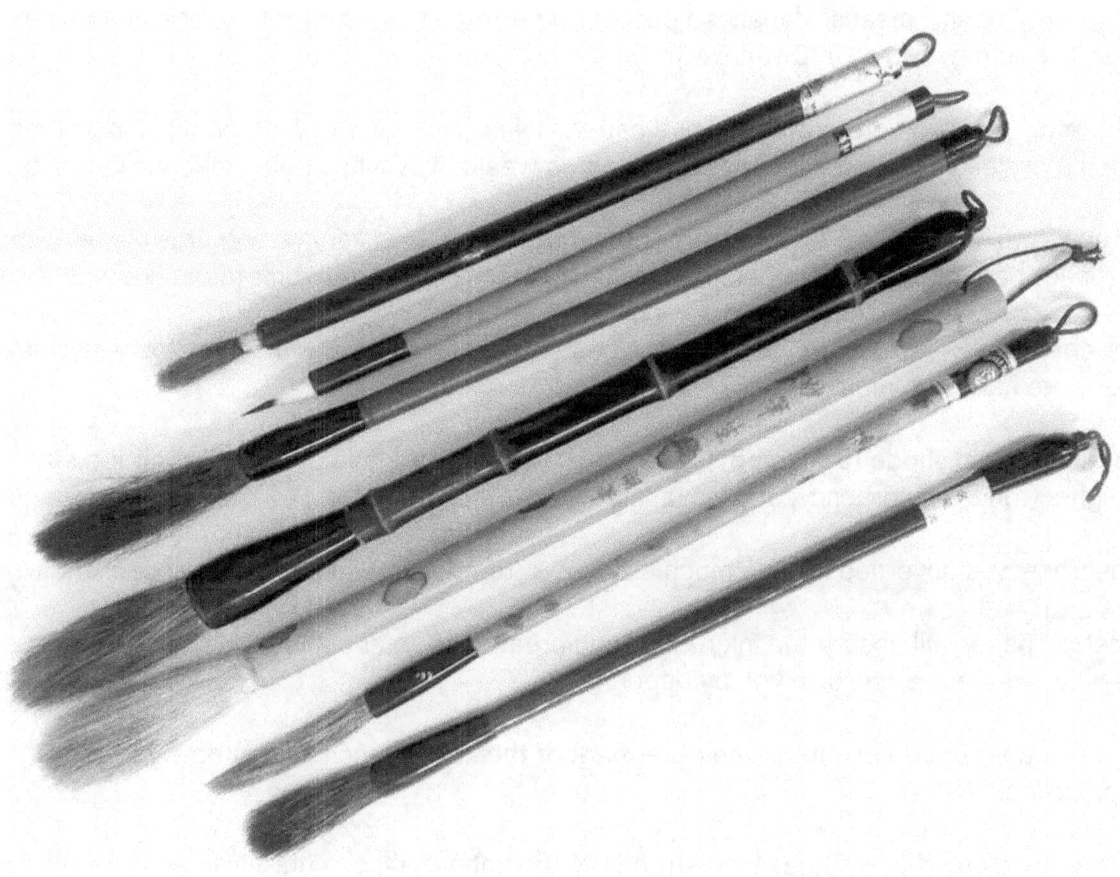

Washi – Japanese Paper

The word "washi" means "Japanese paper" and refers to papers that are still handmade basically as they were 1400 years ago.

The term "washi" is preferable to "rice paper," which is a commonly-used misnomer that gives a misleading impression that the paper is weak. Washi has no connection with rice.

Although thin, translucent and absorbent by nature, washi is very strong. It is made from the inner bark of three renewable bushes — kozo (mulberry), mitsumata, and gampi.

For absorbency, kozo and mitsumata are best; gampi tends to shrink when it is wet, and is therefore harder to manage.

For sumi-e and shodo (calligraphy), there are hundreds of kinds of washi in varying sizes, weights, tones, absorbency, and visual surface.

Absorbency is governed by how much sizing is in the paper, which prevents absorption.

Unsized paper will absorb the ink readily and create soft, blendable brush marks. More heavily-sized paper will give you a crisper line.

"Chiri" paper has small bits of the outer bark of the kozo branch left in the sheet for an organic look.

"Unryu" ("cloud dragon") has long strands of the unbeaten kozo fibre visible in the paper.

The finest "Heritage Washi," made with 100% Japanese kozo or mitsumata, will not change colour over centuries.

If the paper has added wood pulp or has been made with Thai kozo, it may discolour with time.

Gampi is by nature acidic and will darken with age.

One side of washi is smooth, where it has been dried on a wood or steel surface; the other side is rougher, where the brush has laid the wet paper down. Either side of washi can be used.

Unsized paper may have a roughness with little fibres that will catch at the hairs of the brush, creating different textures.

Like good wine, quality washi will become more beautiful and effective with time.

You will come to know the qualities of the various papers through use. As you paint in sumi-e, you may find your preference for either the rough or smooth side, thin or heavier weight, natural or white tone, or one type of paper over another.

The choices are numerous and they are yours!

How to Cut Washi

Traditionally, washi is usually cut in one of two ways.

One can simply wet a clean brush with clear water and draw a fine brushstroke where the paper is to be cut, then gently pull the pieces apart while holding one side immobile.

If this method is used to separate a finished painting from the rest of a sheet or roll of washi, ensure you hold down the side with your finished piece on it and pull on the part you will be discarding, to ensure your painting does not rip in error. This is particularly important if the painting is not quite dry.

The second method is to fold the paper along the line you wish to cut and slip a very sharp knife between the two sides then, while holding the folded paper taut, run the edge along the fold to separate the pieces.

Felt

A piece of white or cream felt is placed to cover your workspace for several reasons.
- It keeps the table clean.
- It helps prevent the paint from spreading uncontrollably on the washi.
- It allows the artists to more clearly see the variations of grays used in the painting.

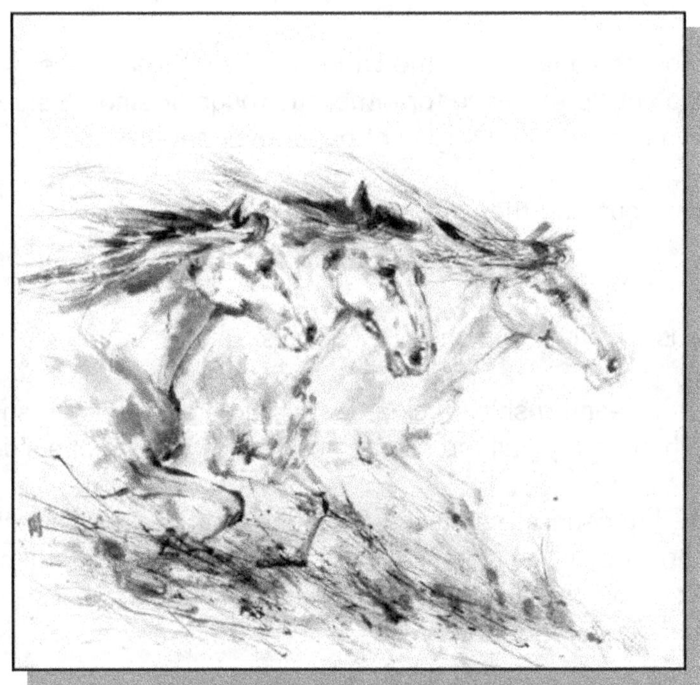

Through High Grass
2017 winner of The Ruth Yamada Award
from Sumi-e Artists of Canada
The meaning of the name stamp is "Play"

Preparing the Ink

Centre yourself while performing this task. All is perfect. The paper is pristine. The brush awaits your hand.

Preparing the ink also creates atmosphere. It is a very important part of the process of painting in sumi-e. Play music that will stimulate your creative process. Create a space where you can be your true self.

Pour a little water into the well — about a tablespoon at most — of the inkstone (suzuri) or onto the surface of one without a well. With the inkstick (sumi) held vertically and flat on the surface of the inkstone, draw some water onto the flat part of the inkstone and, in concentric circles, slowly grind the ink with the water, drawing up more water as needed, until the texture feels silky, smooth and slightly thickened. It is now time to dry all sides of the end of the sumi on your cloth, located just below the suzuri (#7 in the Set-Up), to prevent cracking.

Now you can try the colour of the ink you have produced on your test piece of washi (#10 in the Set-Up). The colour of the ink should be a deep rich black; however, inksticks vary in quality and shade. It is important to wash any leftover ink on your stone at the end of each painting session to ensure that bits of older, dried ink do not impede the smooth texture of the ink you are preparing anew. However, if you have a suzuri with a lid and intend to paint a bit later, you can just place the lid over the ink.

The ink prepared will gradually move back down into the well of the suzuri or, if the suzuri is flat, it will usually settle to one side.

This is not a problem. Just make more black ink as you require it.

DO NOT STOP GRINDING THE INK WITH THE INKSTICK STILL ON THE INKSTONE!

You are creating a vortex, and the inkstick can become so stuck to the inkstone that the effort required to remove sumi from suzuri can result in a broken inkstick!

The ink is used either from the well or the flat area of the inkstone. My preference is to use the ink on the flat portion, as I keep the brush quite dry while painting.

We shall discuss loading the brush in some detail later. For now, you need know simply that you draw the brush gently through the ink, ensuring the hairs of the brush remain straight. Each time you wet the brush with ink or water, use the piece of cloth to remove excess.

Artists should be aware that the ink dries a few shades lighter than it looks when wet.

The mounting method that I use most often brings back the darker look of the ink.

In Japan, the ink is made in the fall. The pine or vegetable matter that will be used is burned, and the resulting charcoal or ash is powdered. This powder is mixed with a glue and the "ink" is then kneaded for hours to incorporate the powder evenly throughout.

The colour of the ink will depend upon the substance used. I use mainly blue-black ink, however there are inks that are green-black, brown-black and other colours as well.

Oils may also be added to scent the sumi beautifully. I find the scent that rises as I grind my ink centres me in preparation for painting.

The kneaded "ink" is packed into molds to dry. These molds may have relief decorations, which can be painted when the inksticks are dry.

Hanko or Name Stamps

The hanko is the artist's signature.

The art of carving hanko is called Tenkoku.

In sumi-e, you are not to use your own hanko until you have received your first name-stamp from your sensei or master.

A hanko can be the 'artist name' chosen for/by that artist which is a reflections of who you are and how you paint. It must both look and sound beautiful.

Hanko can also be words indicative of your style of painting or your response to your images.

Some artists change their artist name many times throughout their career to reflect who they have become, or how their style of painting has changed.

The artist can choose not to sign their name above the hanko as, if they have personally carved it or had it carved for them, it will be unique for that artist.

In Japan, everyone has an official hanko that is used to sign documents, much as we sign our name.

For a sumi-e or shodo artist, the hanko used on a painting is part of the composition of the piece and is placed after the painting is completed.

In shodo, the hanko usually appears on the lower left-hand side of the piece.

In sumi-e, the placement is at the discretion of the artist.

I was awarded my first hanko by Tomoko Kodama early in my sumi-e career. My artist name was decided upon through a two-week period in discussion with my calligraphy sensei, Noriko Maeda. It is "Spring Water" or "Shun Swee."

As of this writing, I have carved over thirty hanko of different sizes and shapes, so I have many choices for each painting. Some of my hanko are my artist name, or just "water" or "spring." I have also carved other words that seemed significant for my paintings, such as "heart/mind/spirit," "elegant" or "journey."

The hanko is carved in wood or rock, usually marble, jade or some kind of agate.

They are carved using steel carving tools, by hand, following a rigorous method developed thousands of years ago.

Hanko are works of art themselves.

Shown here are some of the hanko I have carved over the years.

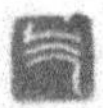 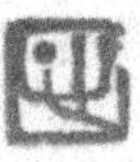 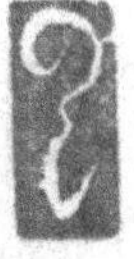 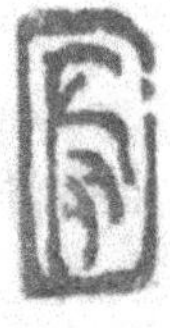 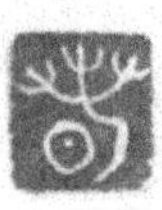  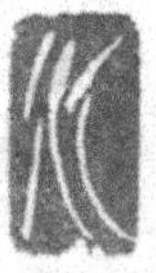 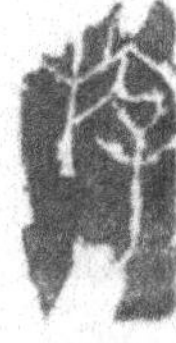

Air/Energy/Ki/Chi   Heart/Mind/Spirit   Cloud   Journey   Spring   Spring Water   Water   Play

How to Hold and Wet Your Brush

To begin, wet the brush by dipping the hairs in clear water and squeezing out the excess using the thumb and first finger. Ensure that the shaft of the brush remains dry, otherwise eventually it may split or the hairs may fall out.

This same process is also used when softening a new brush, when beginning to paint, or when finished painting. In all cases, dip and squeeze until the water runs clear.

To re-shape the tip of the brush, use the edge of your inkstone.

To keep brushes in good shape, travel with them rolled in a bamboo mat or the felt you use under your washi. They can also be hung by the small loop on the end to allow them to dry with the hairs aligned.

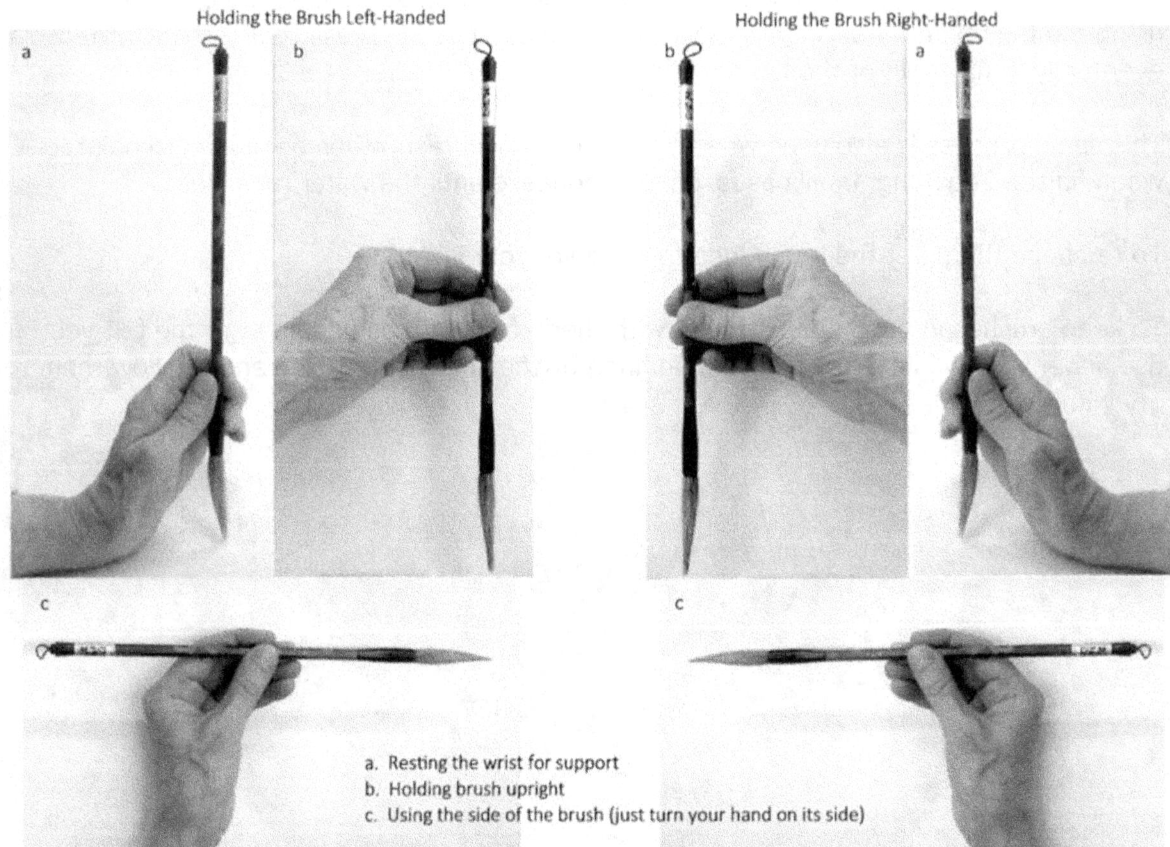

a. Resting the wrist for support
b. Holding brush upright
c. Using the side of the brush (just turn your hand on its side)

Your First Brushstrokes

In painting in the Body, Breath, Brush method, as developed by Tomoko Kodama, the artist does not move the wrist or the arm. Instead, the entire body is involved in the movement. In addition, the artist literally breathes life into each brushstroke.

In sumi-e, your state of mind and spirit are as important as the mastery of technique. Consider that you are not merely painting a picture. Rather than holding the brush in your hand as you paint, you are one with the brush. You become what you are painting. If painting a leaf, for example, feel its stiffness or softness. Feel the warmth of the sun or a dewdrop on its surface.

In order to accomplish this, there are just a few "**rules**" to follow:

- The brush is held in either right or left hand with the thumb on one side and the first three fingers on the other side. It is held gently yet firmly — either straight up and down or on its side, but not slanted.
- To keep your strokes precise as you move, you may rest your wrist on the paper to steady your hand, or use your other hand under your wrist, or to hold the wrist of the hand wielding the brush.
- While painting, do not move your wrist or shoulder. Instead, if standing, the artist shifts their weight from one foot to the other, from heel to toe and side to side, which will allow the brush to move with the body. If seated, the same movement can be accomplished by shifting weight from side to side, or from front to back.
- The head nods down gradually as pressure is applied to the brush tip, and rises as the brush lifts subtly off the paper.
- Breathe into your belly as a baby does, feeling your belly rise and fall. Keep your knees slightly bent and flexible. This is the same "power breathing" used in tai chi and qigong.
- Breathe in before each brushstroke and paint only on an exhale.

- With all brushstrokes, you begin with the brush in the air and end with the brush in the air — whether it is upright or on its side.
- The breath is exhaled as a series of small sounds — such as *ti-ti-ti*, *la-la-la* or *pa-pa-pa* — with varying rhythm, so that each stroke is really a set of interrelated brushstrokes of varying pressures strung together to give the finished brushstroke strength and interest.
- When first performing these strokes, use audible sounds, pushing out more air as pressure is applied, and less air as the brush rises off the paper.
- Bring your brush towards the paper from the direction you will be painting that particular brushstroke.
- As you finish a brushstroke, lift your brush in the direction you are going next with your brush, but do not flick it, as this can be seen in the brushstroke. Bring the brush smoothly off the paper.
- Be aware that usually I use only about the last quarter inch of my brush to paint with. The remainder of the brush serves as a reservoir for my ink. If you apply too much pressure, the brush will become "dishevelled."
- When using the brush horizontally (not to be confused with the Horizon brushstroke), draw your hand across the paper with the length of the brush touching the washi.
- Place the free hand gently upon the felt to provide balance, grounding and centering of your spirit.

Refer back to this page each time you are about to paint until these "rules" are a part of you!

Basic Brushstrokes

In traditional teaching, one is taught that there are eight brushstrokes, all of which are contained in the work for "eternity," shown here.

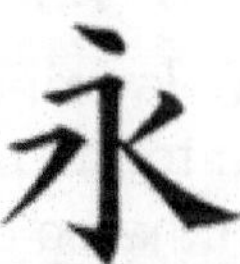

I will describe three brushstrokes from which all those in "Eternity" can be created.

Once you have practiced these brushstrokes many times — on their own or as part of several paintings — and become proficient in the rise and fall of the brush, you will find that with each brushstroke, you will breathe Life into your images!

Until you have read through "Loading the Brush," do not concern yourself with getting the shading perfected while first practicing the three brushstrokes described on the following pages.

***With all brushstrokes, please be mindful of your breathing and movement as described in "Your First Brushstrokes"**

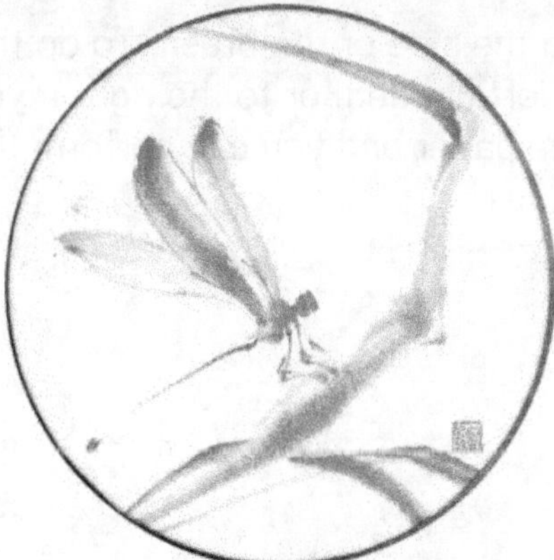

On a Broken Reed by author
Hanko is "Spring Water" - author's artist name

Horizon Brushstroke

The first brushstroke I will refer to as the "Horizon" brushstroke simply because, when painted horizontally, it looks like the horizon of a landscape.

Holding the brush vertically, breathe in. While exhaling, begin moving in the direction you are going to paint while lowering the brush to the paper. When the brush first touches the paper, keep moving and apply pressure on the tip of the brush. As you apply pressure, nod your head down, breathe out more vigorously and, if you are standing, bend your knees — all of which will incorporate more of your spirit in your brushstroke. As you continue moving your brush, lessen the pressure on the brush (raise your head, breathe less vigorously and, if standing, straighten your knees) and raise the brush, while moving, until just one hair is on the paper and then, finally, the brush is completely off the paper.

The more pressure applied, the wider the brushstroke will be. The wetter the brush, the wider the brushstroke will be. The more absorbent the paper, the wider the brushstroke will be.

This brushstroke can be performed in every direction. The brushstroke can be curved or straight, long or short.

Next try this brushstroke using the side of the brush. To do this, turn your hand holding the brush to the left if you are left-handed, or to the right if you are right-handed. The brush will now be parallel to the paper and you can perform the brushstroke as described above.

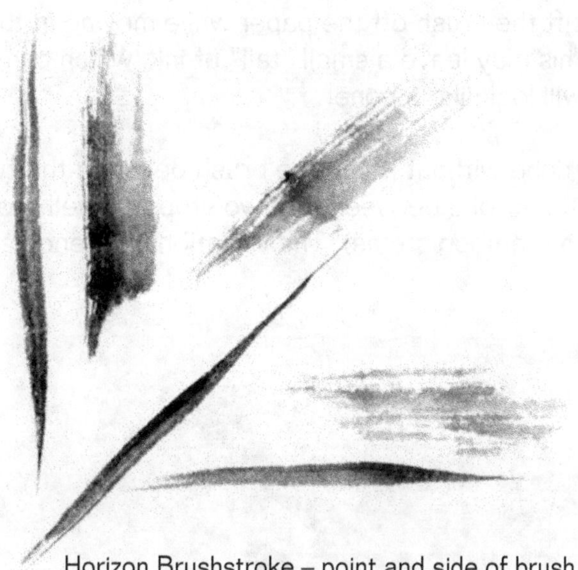

Horizon Brushstroke – point and side of brush

Bone Stroke

As with the Horizon brushstroke, hold the brush upright; breathe in and, while exhaling, begin moving in the direction you are going to paint while lowering the brush to the paper.

When the brush touches the paper, stop a moment with a puff of breath, lift the brush slightly off the paper and quickly across it, and then stop at the end of the stroke with another puff of breath. Lift the brush off the paper while moving in the direction the next brushstroke will begin. This may leave a small "tail" of ink, which can be quite lovely. The completed brushstroke will look like a bone!

This brushstroke can be done without lifting the brush between the two stops at beginning and end. You can curve the stroke between the two stops as well. You can try painting with the side of the brush (bamboo stems). The variations are endless.

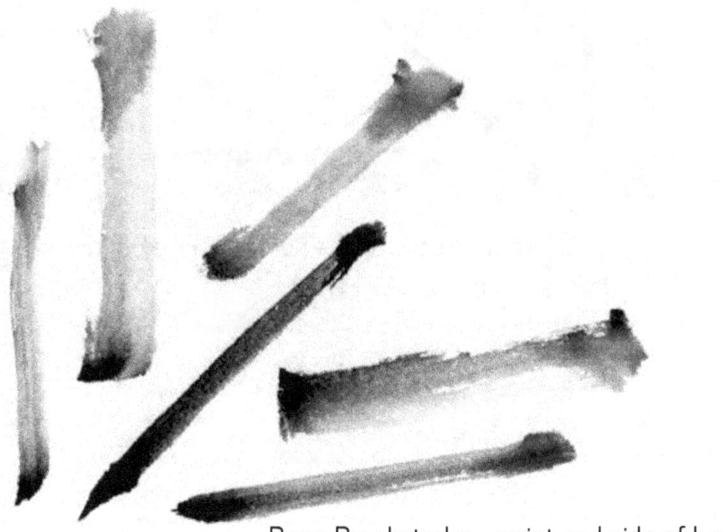

Bone Brushstroke – point and side of brush

Dot

In one of the Chinese brush painting books I have, the author speaks of there being many ways of painting the "Dot." However, upon closer examination, some were the same brushstroke performed in different directions. I will describe that Dot as well as two other methods for painting dots, all of which are useful.

Method 1: With the brush held vertically, take a breath in. Bring the brush down to the paper as though painting the Horizon stroke. Exhale and pause the brush for a microsecond with a puff of breath, then gradually lift the brush up off the paper while moving back the way you came into the brushstroke. The brushstroke will look like a little tadpole. Practice this brushstroke in all directions. Also practice curving the brushstroke as you lift the brush.

Method 2: With the brush held vertically, take a breath in. Bring the brush down, moving from left to right. After you have made a short "tail" (that is, after the brush has actually touched the paper), pause the brush with a puff of breath and lift the brush up while moving back to the left, but slightly lower than you entered the brushstroke while exhaling, again producing a small tail. This brushstroke may look a bit like a little bird.

Method 3: With the brush held vertically, take a breath in. Bring the brush down to the paper while beginning to move in a circular direction. Once your brush touches the paper, continue to circumscribe a circle, gently lifting the brush at the completion of the circle while still moving in a circular direction.

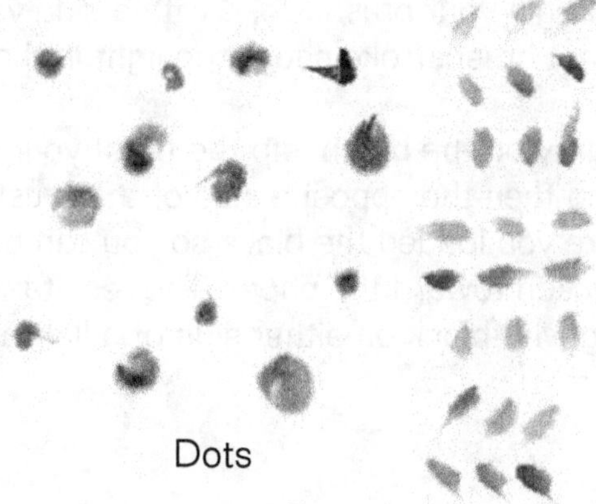

Dots

Loading the Brush

In sumi-e, a multitude of grays are incorporated into each brushstroke by using different loading techniques. Using the strokes you have just practiced, add variations by loading the brush with grays, as described below.

For each method below, begin by loading your brush with only a light gray. To do this:
- Draw your brush through the black ink.
- Touch the water in your white dish with your brush.
- Remove excess on the cloth and test the colour on the scrap of washi.
- If you believe it is too dark a gray, again touch the side of the brush to the water and remove excess water with the cloth before testing once more.

Different methods of loading the brush:
a) Just light gray on the brush.
b) Beginning with light gray on the brush, dip just the tip of your brush in the pure black on the "plateau" of your inkstone. Remove excess water with your cloth. Your brushstroke should be dark at the beginning and then fade to a lighter gray
c) Beginning with light gray on the brush, draw the side of your brush through the black ink on the "plateau" of the inkstone and remove excess water on the cloth. Your finished brushstroke should be dark along one side.
d) Beginning once more with light gray on the brush, draw first one side and then the other through the black ink on your inkstone, keeping track of where you loaded the black so you can begin your brushstroke with a side you did not blacken toward the paper. The resultant brushstroke should be light in the middle and darker along the sides.
e) Beginning with light gray on the brush, dip the tip of your brush in black ink, then draw first one side and then the opposite side of the brush through the black ink, keeping track of where you loaded the black so you can begin the brushstroke with a side you did not blacken toward the paper. The resultant brushstroke should be black at the beginning with black on either side of a lighter gray part.

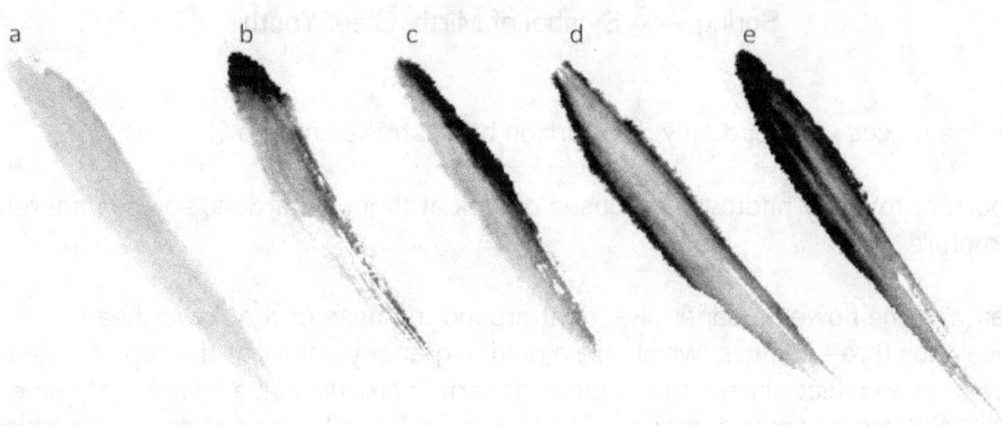

a) gray
b) gray with black on the tip
c) gray with black down one side
d) gray with black on two sides
e) gray with black on the tip and
   two sides

Crocus
Spring — A Symbol of Mirth, Glee, Youth

To paint the crocus you need only the Horizon brushstroke and the Dot.

It is important to study photos of crocuses or look at them in gardens so you understand their structure.

The sheath of the flower is paper-like; tight around the base of the flower head.
The crocus has three stigmas, which are a golden orangey colour at the top of a slender stem. Saffron is collected from the stigmas of certain crocuses. Be aware that some crocus species are poisonous, though. The leaves are usually straight and to the sides of the flower but can also bend outward from the base of the flower, especially in older flowers. All grow out of the corm that has wintered under the ground. You can cross the leaves, but not all at the sa-me point.

When painting, this as with any subject, do not think of painting petal – petal – petal – sheath – leaf – leaf – leaf. Rather, paint Flower! Feel the stiffness of this succulent little plant. Feel the cold earth and the snow on your feet, and the warmth of the sun on your face. Become each part of this plant as you paint it!

Flower Head

First put a dot of water on the paper to indicate the centre of the flower. You will aim for the centre with each petal brushstroke, but you need not ever reach it.

Load your brush with light gray with a darker shade on the side of the brush. You can, alternatively, put a few shades of purple on your brush, or a purple and a gray, or a few shades of yellow, or yellow and gray.

- Using the side of the brush, take a deep breath in and move the brush upwards on the page until you touch the paper. Then, begin to move down the paper, applying pressure and then gently raising the brush while angling it so that less of the brush is in contact with the paper, ending with a soft edge. The up-down movement softens the top of the petal. For a bud or a flower just opening, begin the second petal using less of the side of the brush, and with a bit of a space between the petals. For a flower that is not fully open, you can have two to four petals with the whole looking semi-closed.
- You can paint the same petals but without brushing up before rushing downwards. Painting in this manner, it can be more difficult to have a soft entry into the petal.
- For a more open flower, look at your photos or at actual flowers and follow the curved shape you see.
- Whether the flower is just barely open or fully opened, one or two petals can be painted as though behind by lifting the brush at the end of the stroke, so that the petal is behind and does not touch any others.

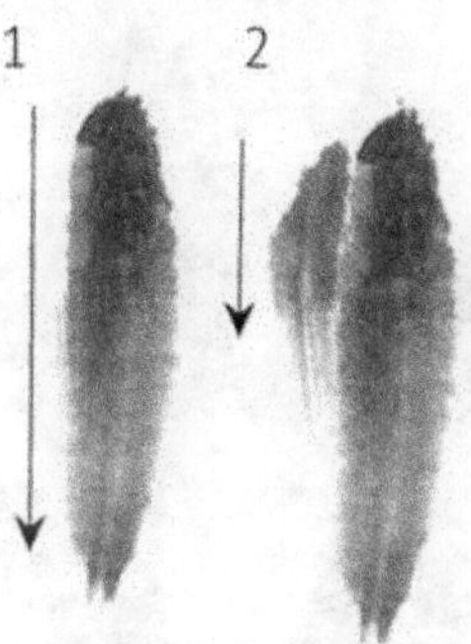

Anthers & Stigma

The anthers, surrounded by the stigmas, grow out of the centre of the flower head. In the crocus there are three — actually a set of three Dots on a long thin stem. If you see them at all, it is usually only the top of this part of the flower.

If you choose to paint the anthers, you can place only one at its centre, if you wish. The viewer's imagination will fill in the rest.

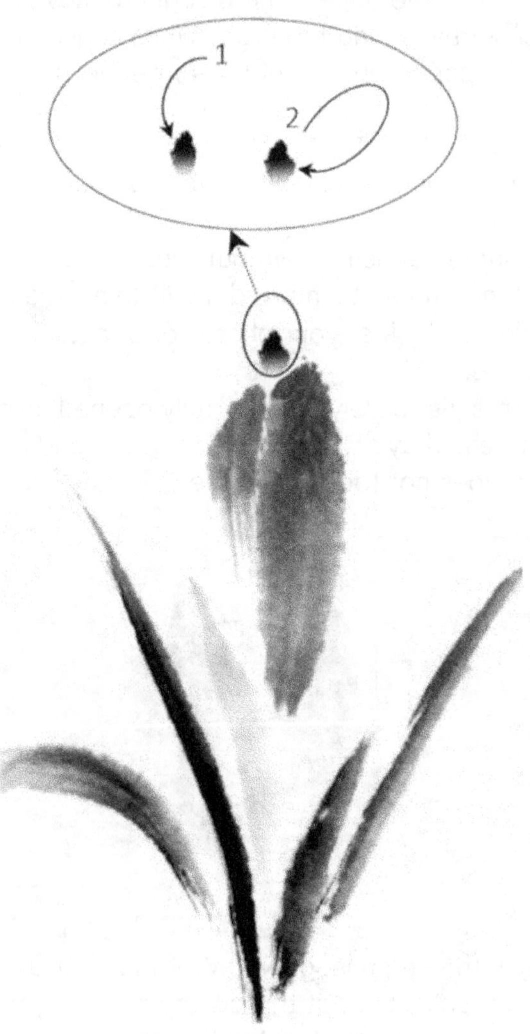
1
2

Sheath and Leaves

The sheath is several layers of thin papery sheets around the base of the flower and the top of the stem.

To paint the sheath, use the Horizon stroke with your brush vertical. Begin in the air and touch the paper to the side of the base of the petals, though not touching the petals. Apply a slight amount of pressure and gently lift the brush at just past the bottom of the petals.

I usually begin painting the leaves from the base of the flower on the ground, and usually think of them as growing out of the snow, as I always saw them on Parliament Hill in Ottawa in early spring. They can, however, be painted from the tip of each leaf instead — whichever feels more comfortable for you. This again is a Horizon brushstroke, however very thin with a white line down the centre of each. You can use two brushstrokes for each leaf, although I tend not to do this.

Beginning in the air, bring the brush down at the base of where the flower would be growing out of the ground. When the brush touches down, it need not be pointed. Think of it as emerging from the dirt or snow and growing almost straight upwards, not quite as tall as the flower-head itself. Remembering that all the leaves are growing out of the corm below the soil, the leaves should begin quite close together and grow upwards, straight or leaning away from the flower and ending in a point.

Refer to photos of a real crocus to get the idea of the construction of the flower and its leaves.

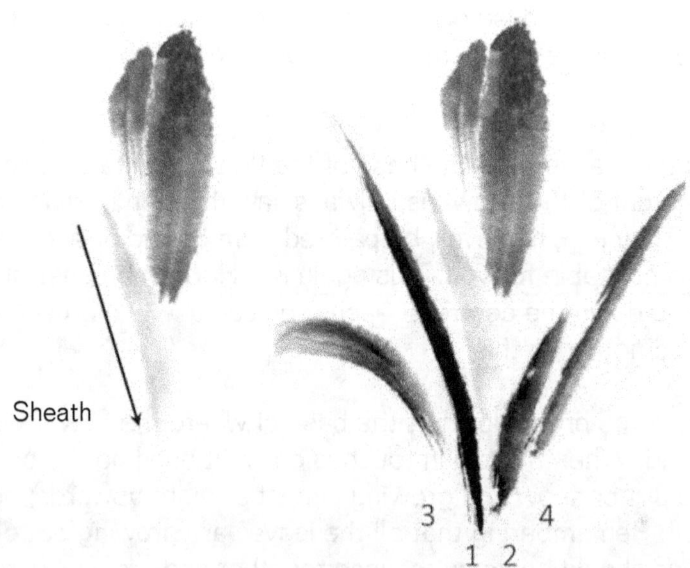

Using the brushstroke order shown, begin either at
the tip or base of the leaf

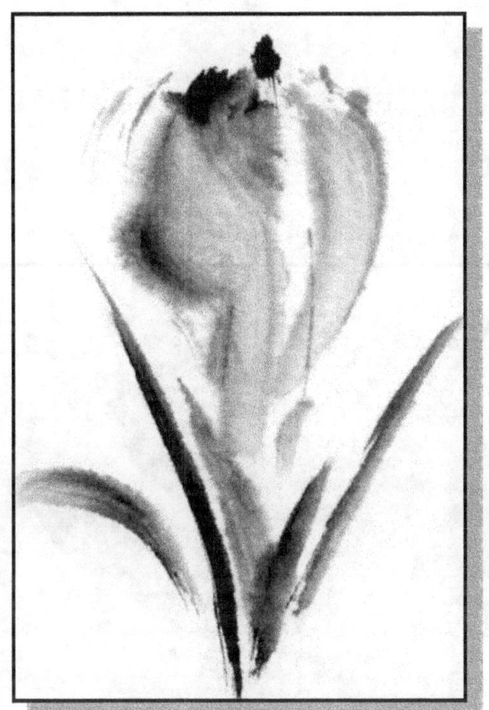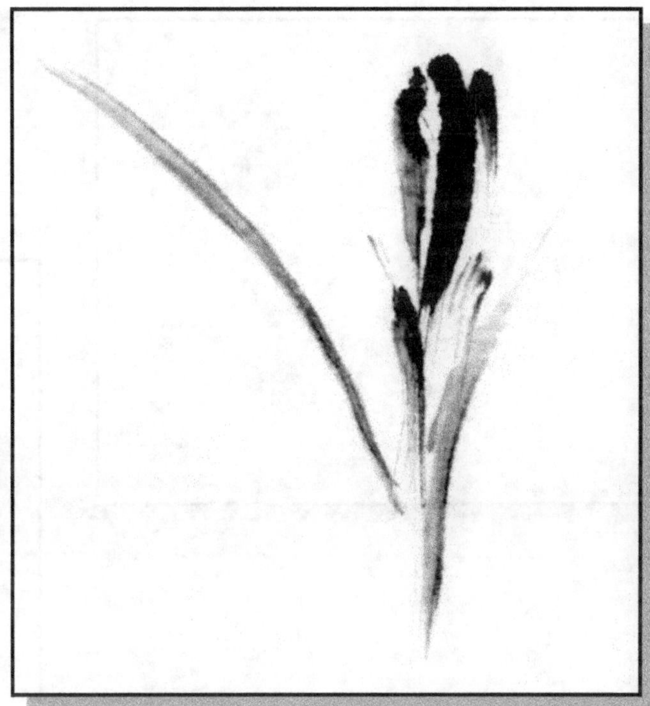

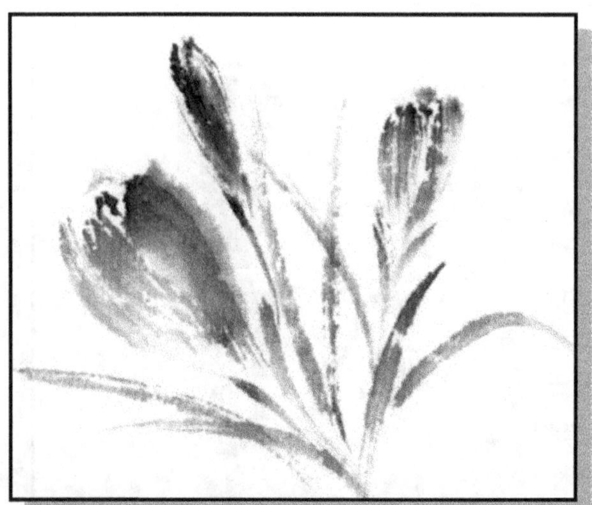

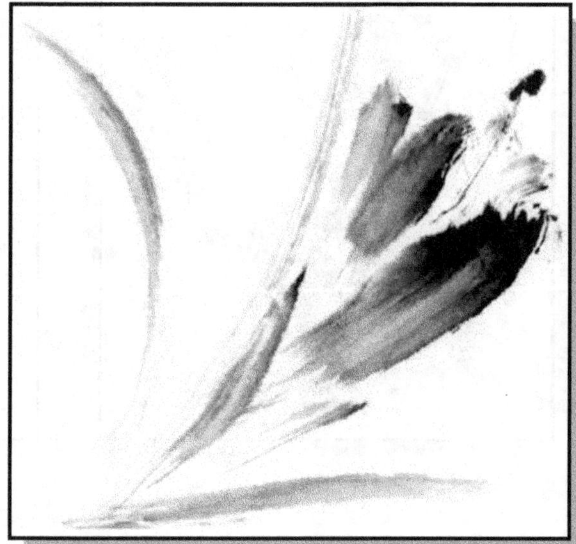

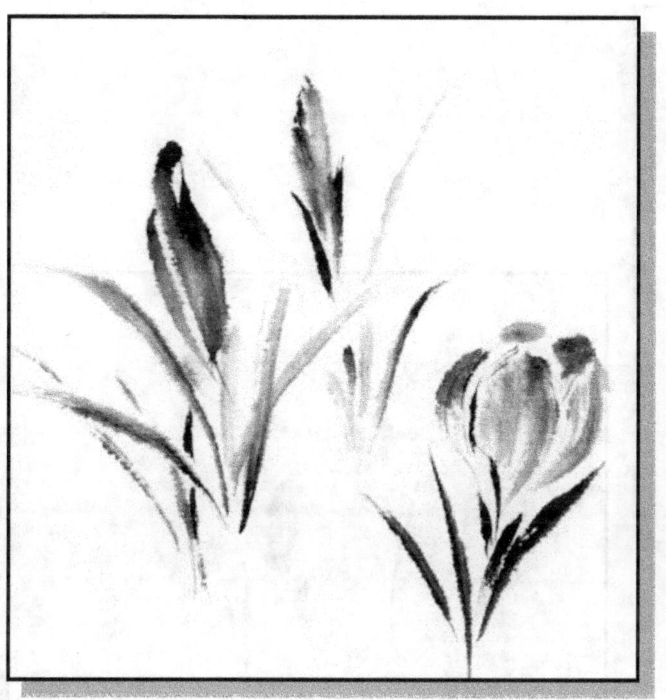

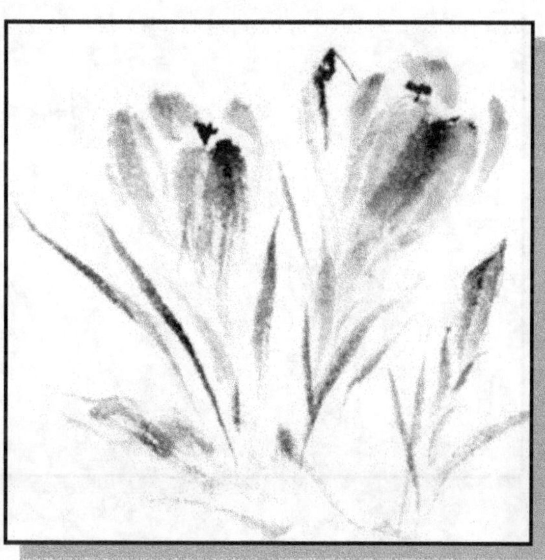

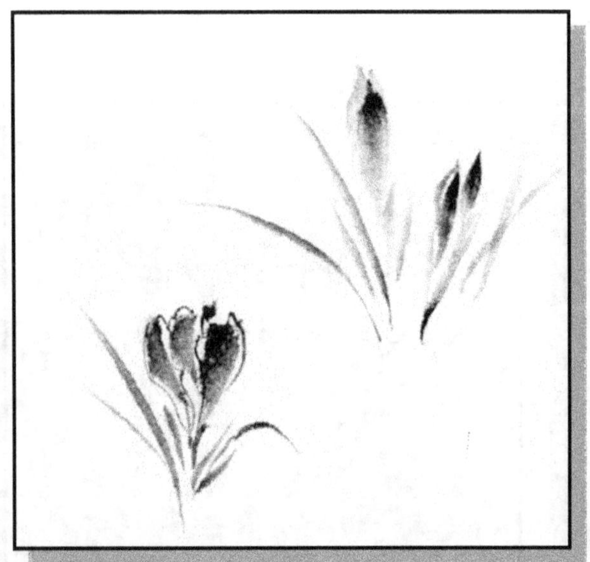

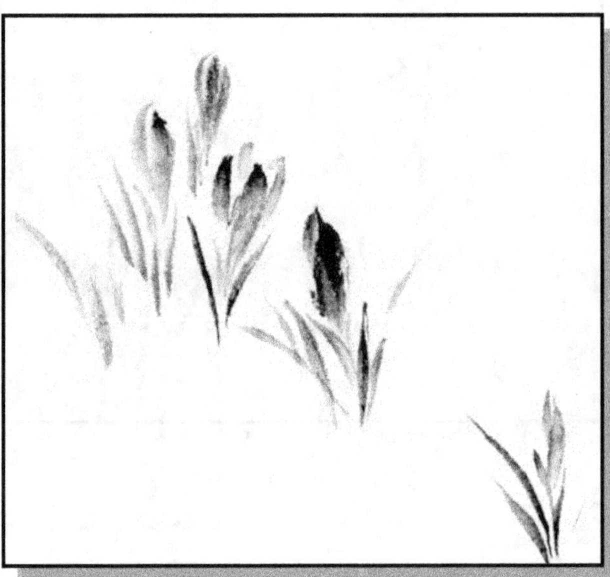

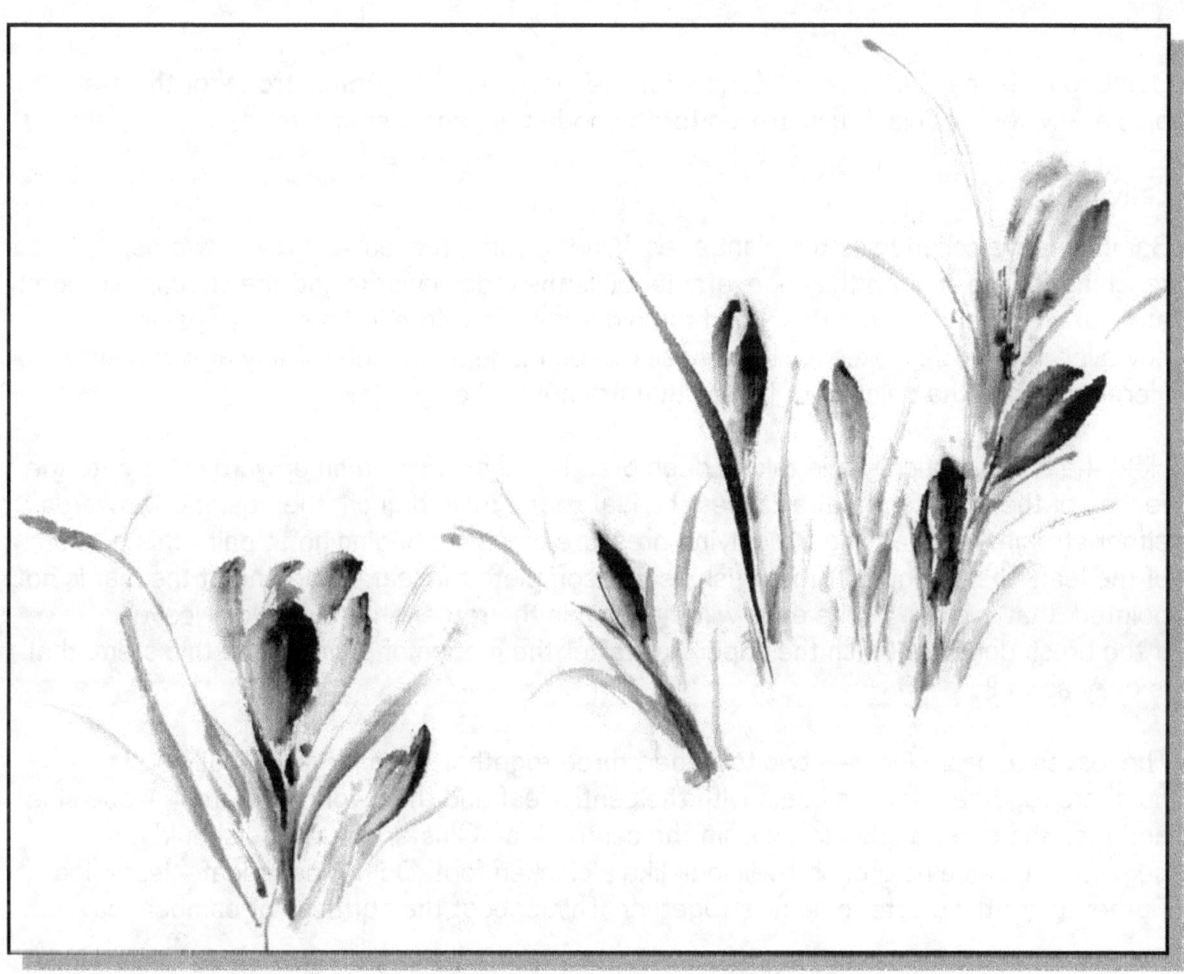

Bamboo
Summer — A Symbol of Virtue and Culture

Bamboo uses the Horizon brushstroke for the leaves and the Bone stroke for the stem, plus a few very special brushstrokes for the node between stem parts.

Leaves

Bamboo leaves change as the plant ages. When young, the leaves grow upwards, reaching for the sun. As they age, gravity pulls them downwards and they become ragged at what were very pointed tips. I find the older bamboo more interesting to paint myself; however, the brushstrokes for the leaves can be made as though for any age of plant. Here I describe the painting of leaves that are not in their youth.

Hold the brush vertically and take a deep breath. Exhale and brush upwards to create the feeling of the thin stem that attaches the leaf to the main branch, then paint downwards, either straight or on an angle, applying pressure just after beginning to paint this portion of the leaf. Then, gently lift the brush as you complete the leaf. If the end of the leaf is not pointed, that is okay, as the ends will then mimic the rather shredded older leaves. If the brush does not touch the paper until after the motion of painting the thin stem, that is okay as well.

The leaves appear singly — two together, three together, or in larger, usually odd numbers together. Always begin with the centre leaf and then work outwards — one side and then the other angled away from the central leaf. Clusters of leaves should not all begin at the same height, or it will look like a chicken foot! Do not paint leaf – leaf – leaf. Rather, paint the cluster of leaves together. Think about the stiffness of bamboo leaves.

You can use overlapping sets of three leaves where each set is a different shade of gray, creating the feeling of three dimensions. The leaves can be curved to indicate bamboo in the wind; however, remember to angle the leaves in the same direction — unless, of course, they are in a tornado or cyclone, and thus moving in all directions at once!

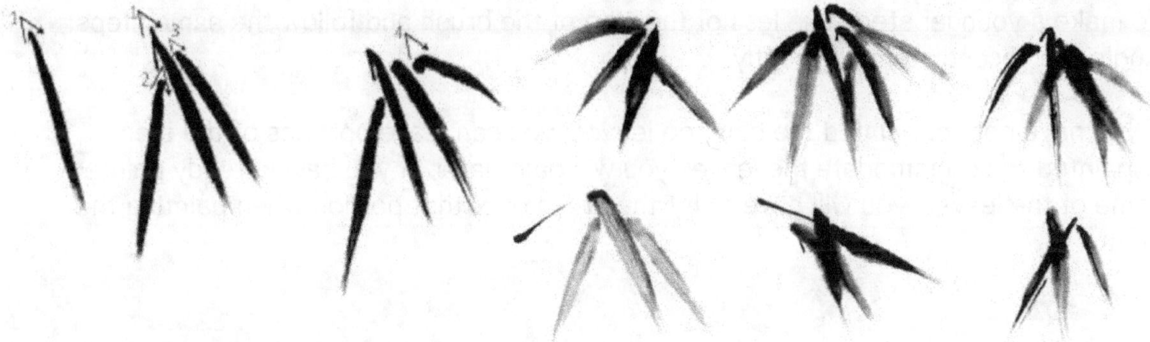

Feel the stiffness of the leaves.

When painting more than two leaves in a cluster,
begin in the middle and paint the following leaves by
alternating the sides they are painted on.

Branches or Stems

The Chinese will portray three stems of varying widths, which they consider to be the
Grandfather, Father and Son. This is certainly something to consider when you compose a
piece of artwork.

Load your brush with light gray and put black on the tip. You will probably have to renew
the black before painting each portion of the stem. Paint all stems beginning at the base.
For the widest stem paint the Bone stroke using the side of the whole brush.

Take a deep breath and bring the side of the brush down to the paper — stop a moment
— lift the brush a bit and move quickly upwards for the length of this portion of stem —
stop a moment — lift the brush, moving it back toward the base of the stem. Load a bit of
black on the tip. Leave a tiny space between the next portion of stem and the one already
painted, and paint it in the same manner but of a different length. For the last portion of
the stem, begin as usual, leaving a tiny space for the node, but instead of doing the final
"stop a moment," lift the brush gently and totally off the page so it appears the stem goes
on forever.

To make a younger stem, use less of the side of the brush and follow the same steps. Angle the second stem differently.

If you have not yet painted the bamboo leaves, you can leave portions of the stem unpainted to accommodate the leaves you will paint later. If you have already painted some of the leaves, you will have to lift the brush over that portion when painting the stem.

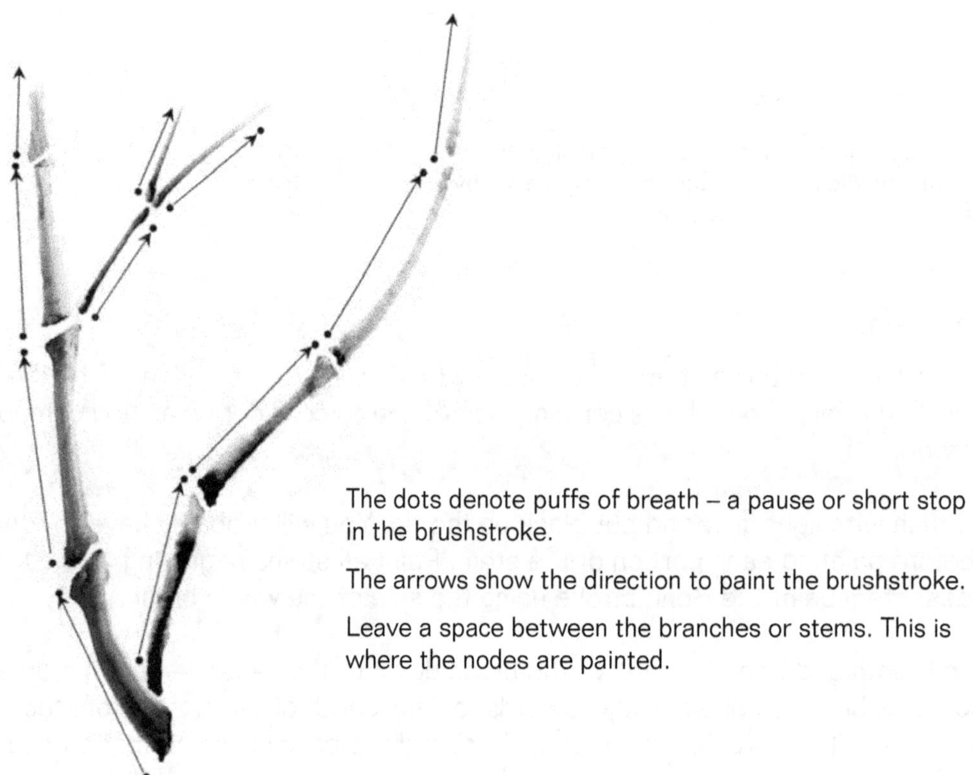

The dots denote puffs of breath – a pause or short stop in the brushstroke.

The arrows show the direction to paint the brushstroke.

Leave a space between the branches or stems. This is where the nodes are painted.

Nodes

The nodes are seen in the spaces between the Bone strokes painted for the stem.
If you look at a piece of bamboo, you will see them. It appears as though the two Bone
stroke portions were pushed together at the joint, creating the node.

There are several ways to paint the nodes between the portions of the stem. When
painting any nodes, they can be outside the stem area on both sides, and can also go
above and/or below the space left for the node. This will make them look more natural.

For young bamboo, you use a "smiley." To do this, you will paint a tiny Bone stroke that
forms an upward curve between the stops, looking like a smile.

- Bring the brush gently down and pause a moment.
- Lift the brush a bit and, moving quickly, form a smile shape with the brush tip.
- Pause a moment before lifting the brush off the page.

For older bamboo, there are a few options:
- A set of brushstrokes looking a bit like a cup. Begin with the Horizon stroke coming
  down and curved a bit outwards. Stop and paint a Bone stroke, curved a bit like a
  frown. Then stop and finish with a Horizon stroke going up and a bit outwards.
- A set of brushstrokes that looks a bit like a frog's mouth. Bring the brush down
  and stop a moment, then paint a bone stroke that goes up to the left then turns
  and comes back to be level with where you first touched down. Touch down a
  moment again before lifting the brush off the page.
- Combining the first two styles but with a twist, begin with the Horizon stroke
  coming down and curved a bit outwards — stop a moment — then paint a Bone
  stroke that goes up to the left then turns and comes back to be level with where
  you first touched down. Touch down a moment before finishing with a Horizon
  stroke moving downward.

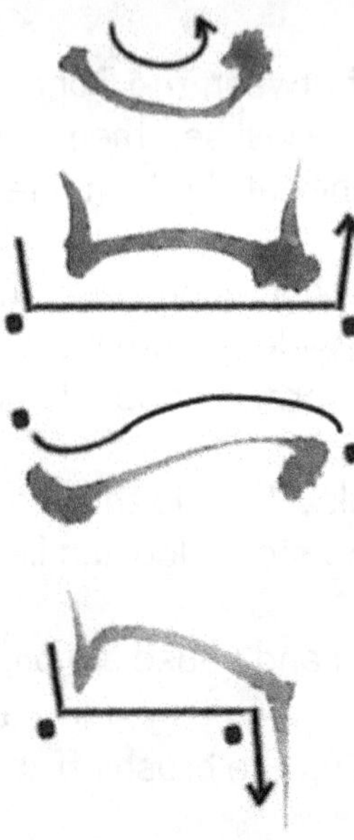

The top style of node is usually for younger stems;
however, they all can be used anywhere
that they look natural.

Bamboo Painting Step-by-Step

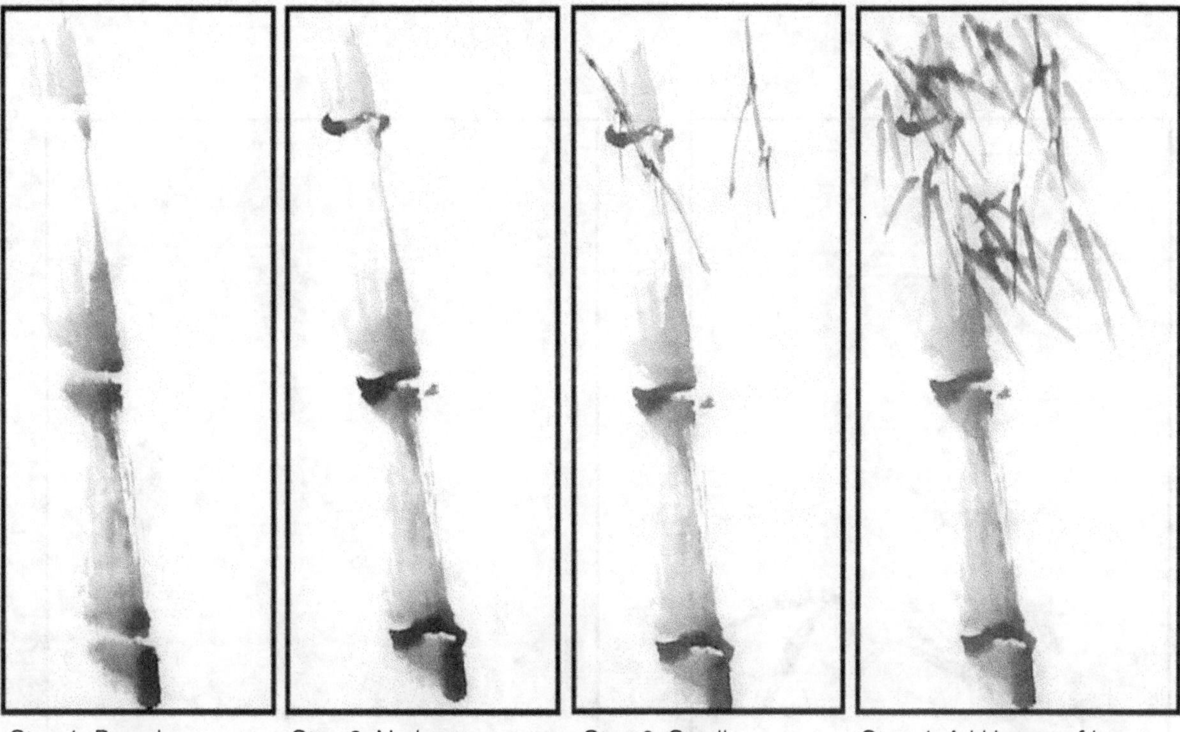

Step 1: Branches

Step 2: Nodes

Step 3: Smaller branches added

Step 4: Add layers of leaves

Steps 3 and 4 are interchangeable. That is, you can add leaves and other branches in any order as you form your composition.

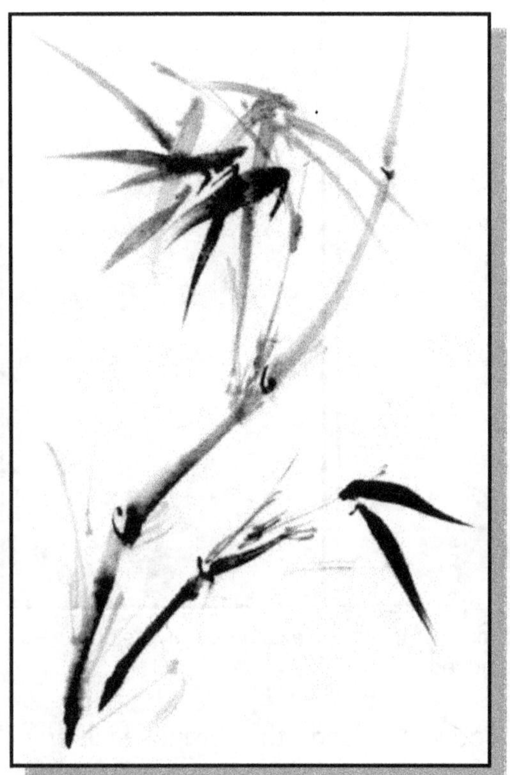
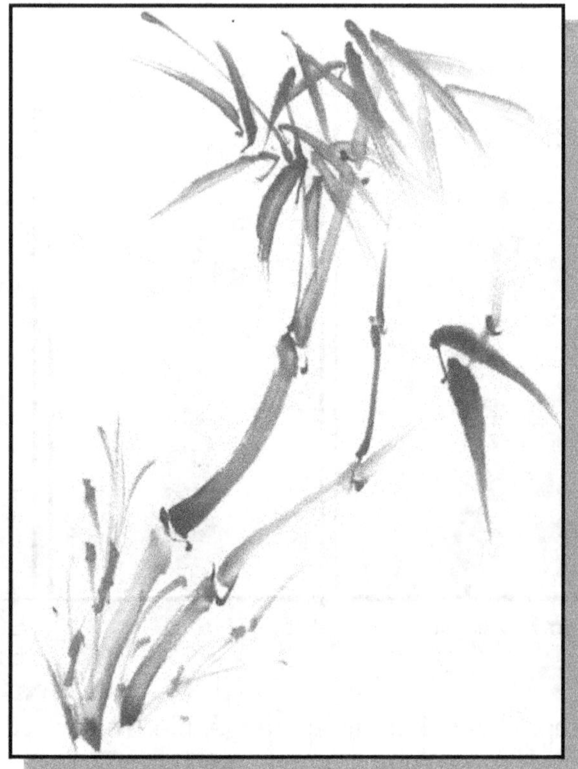

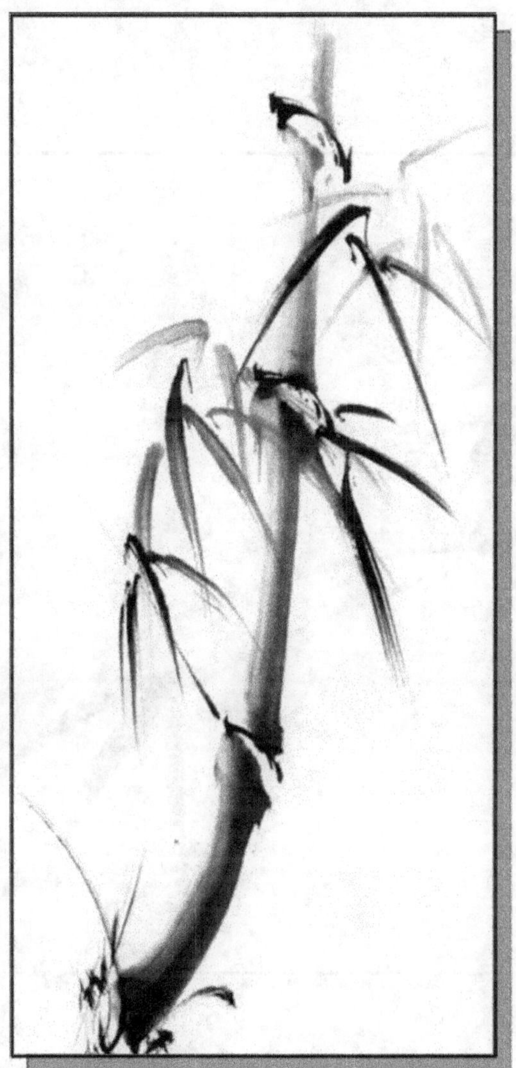

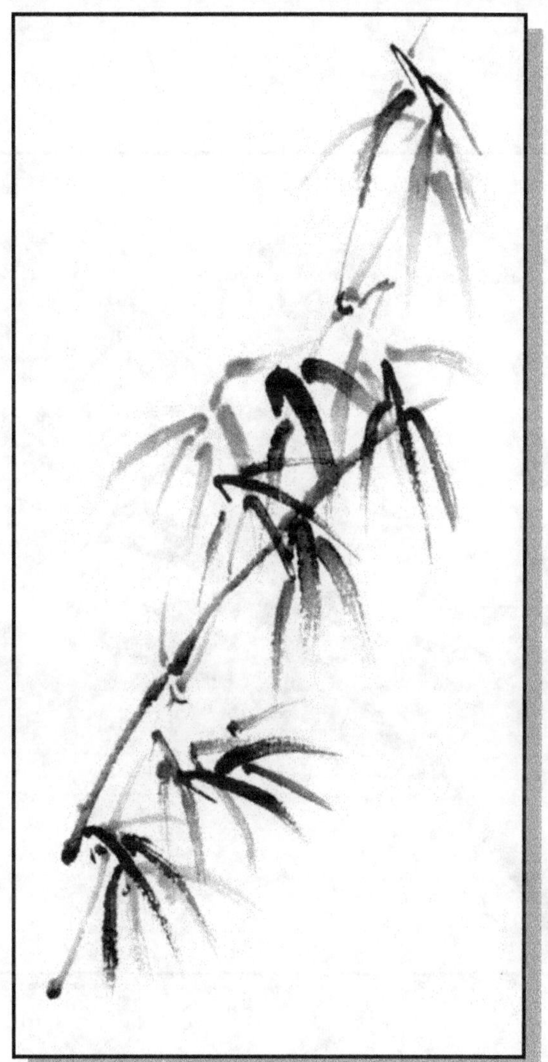

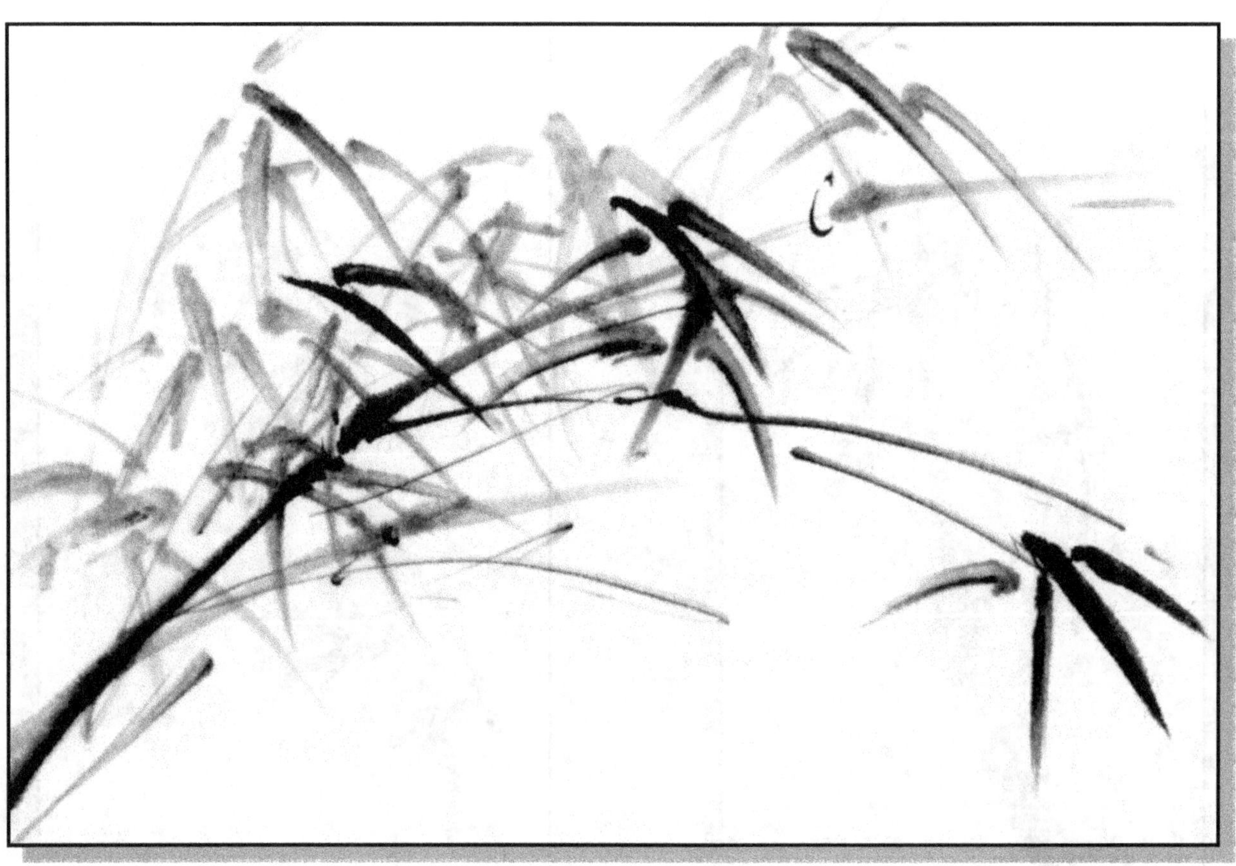

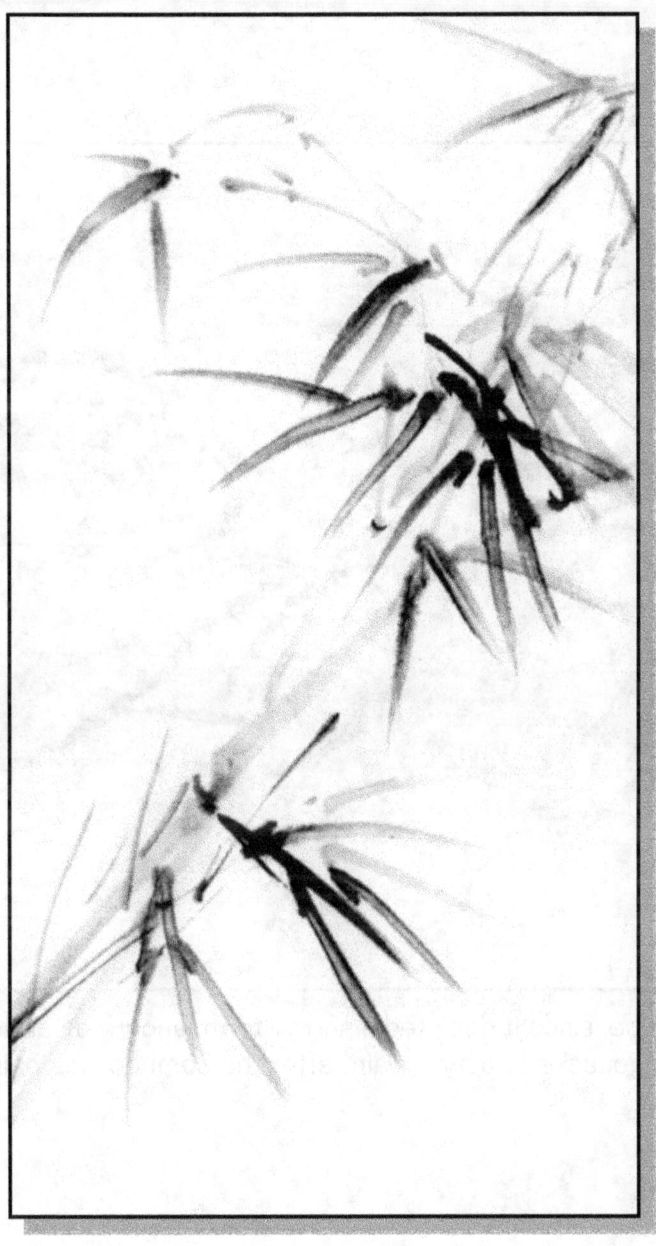

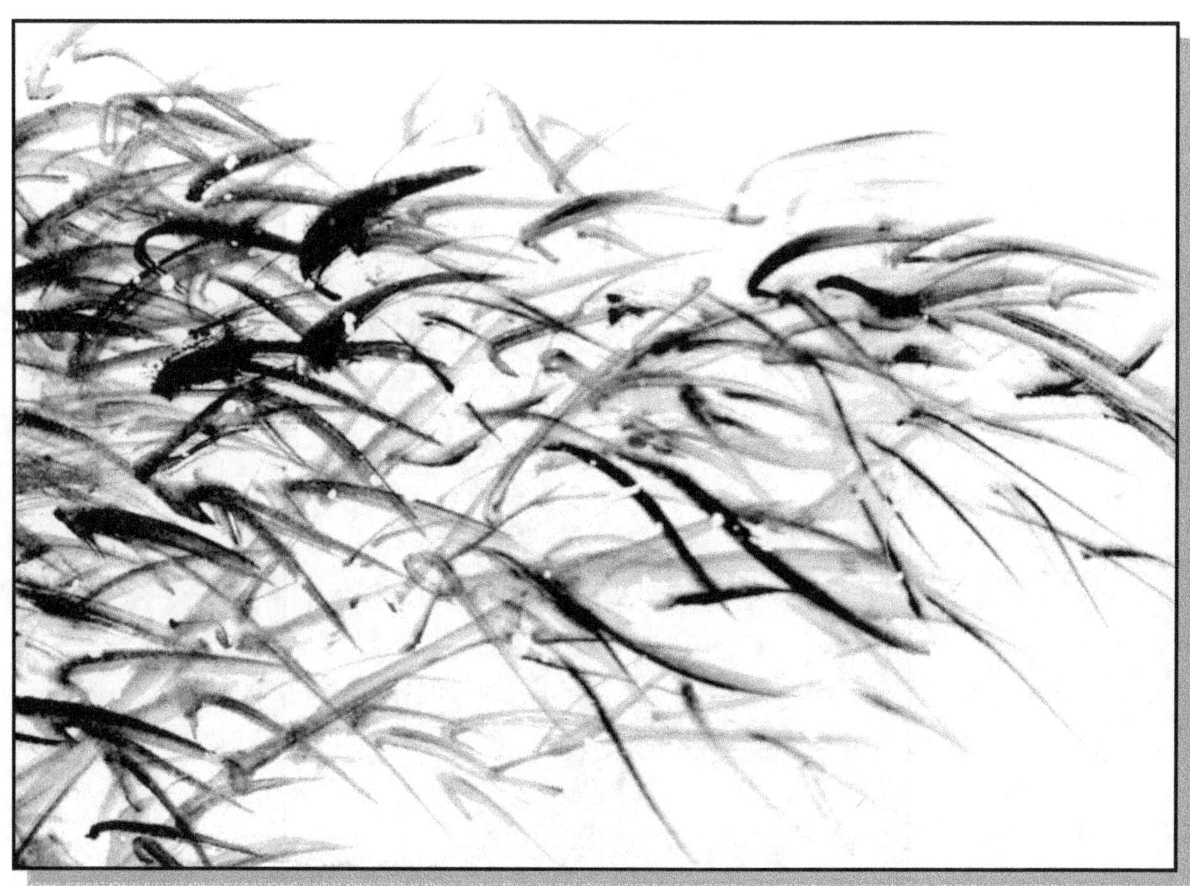

In this piece, since it depicted a snow storm, snow was added using
white gouache or acrylic paint after the bamboo was painted.

Pear
Symbolism — In China, the Pear represents Immortality and Prosperity; In Korea, the Pear represents Grace, Nobility and Purity

I love painting pears and made them a part of my beginner's courses to help students understand the rise and fall of the brush, which is useful in painting so many subjects.

The outside of the pear can be painted in one brushstroke from the tip of the stem all the way around the fruit; however, first let us separate the stem portion from the fruit itself.

Stem

The stem is painted with the Bone stroke and can show a great deal of character in its form.
- Brush upright — inhale — then bring the brush down to the paper with a puff of breath.
- Lift the brush so just a bit of the tip is still on the paper.
- Move very quickly and describe your stem. It can be long and curved (Bosc pear), or short and stubby (Anjou). It can have a break in it.
- Samples can be seen below.
- Bring the brush down with a puff of breath to mark the end of the stem.

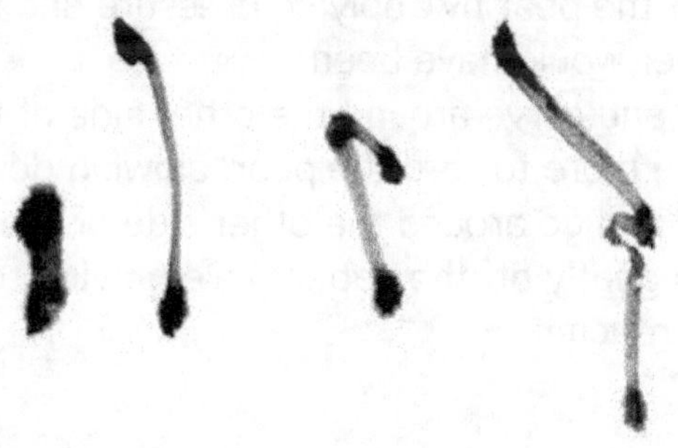

Around the Fruit

The portion of the pear that is the actual fruit can be a continuation of the stem or painted separately.

Following the ideal of a painting in just one brushstroke, I suggest continuing from the end of the stem in an actual painting. In this exercise, we will paint just the fruit. However, the numbering of the steps will show that this is, indeed, a continuation of the same brushstroke.

The pear is a very sensual shape, rather like the torso and hips of a woman.

Consider the shape of the pear as a triangle with an oval on the top.

When painting a pear, at the joins of triangle and oval — the "hip" — and at the bottom centre of the triangle, slow down and apply pressure toward the inside of the brush without turning the brush inwards toward the body of the pear.

- Brush upright — inhale — then bring the brush down to the paper with a puff of breath.
- Lift the brush slightly and curve around the top of the pear (oval area) quickly. When you reach the "hip," apply pressure leaning more toward the pear and slow down.
- Lift the brush slightly and, moving quickly, curve around to the bottom of the pear.
- Ground the bottom of the pear by applying pressure and slowing down for the calyx (where the flower would have been).
- Lift the brush slightly and curve around the other side of the pear to the "hip" and apply pressure leaning more toward the pear, slowing down.
- Lift the brush slightly and go around the other side of the "oval" portion of the pear, lifting the brush gently off the paper while moving toward the base of the stem, but before you reach it.

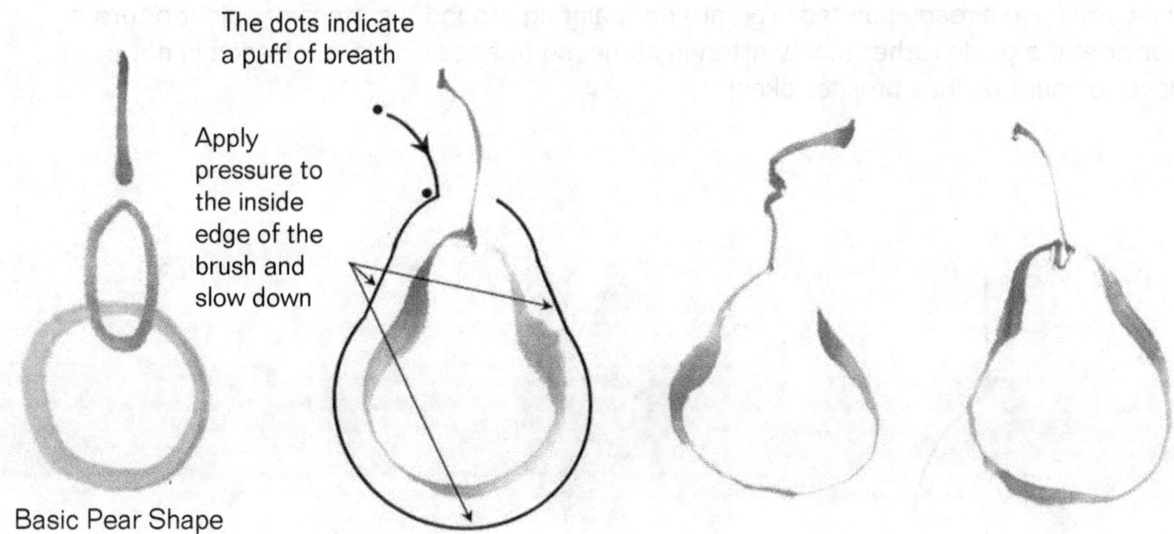
The dots indicate
a puff of breath
Apply
pressure to
the inside
edge of the
brush and
slow down
Basic Pear Shape

Massing in the Pear Shape

Before painting the pear at all, you can mass in the shape of the pear with several shades of gray, or two colours, on your brush. To do this, load your brush with a few colours. They do not have to be true pear colours. Have fun! Perhaps blue and purple or gold and green. With the side of the brush, quickly mass in the shape of the pear without being overly accurate with the shape.

After doing this, paint the stem and around the fruit without paying close attention to what you have already painted. You are not painting around the mass of colour or grays. Consider it a guide rather than written in stone, so to speak. This is a lesson in not being a slave to your previous brushstrokes!

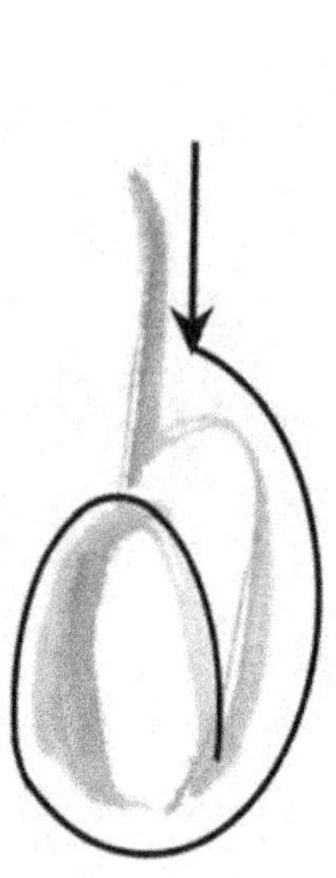

Path of the brush for massing in shape using side of brush with Horizon Brushstroke

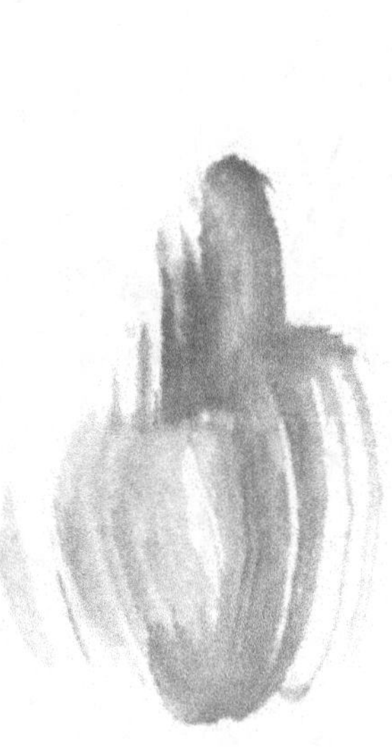

Massed in Pear

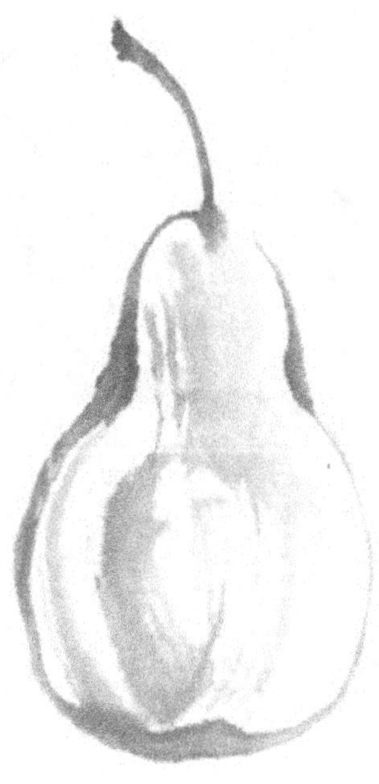

Paint around massed in area as described in previous image.
** Do not follow the mass precisely.

A Cut Pear

If you have not massed in the shape of the pear first, your painting will be completed or you can paint the inside of the pear.

To paint the inside of the pear:
- First paint the centre core of the pear from the stem to the calyx using a Bone stroke, moving quickly.
- Next come the seed areas, for which the Bone stroke is also used in three parts on either side of the centre line, each forming the top, side and bottom of the seed area. Both should be slightly different shapes — definitely not squared off, but rather skewed.
- Inside each seed area, place one or perhaps two seeds using the Dot, slightly curved.

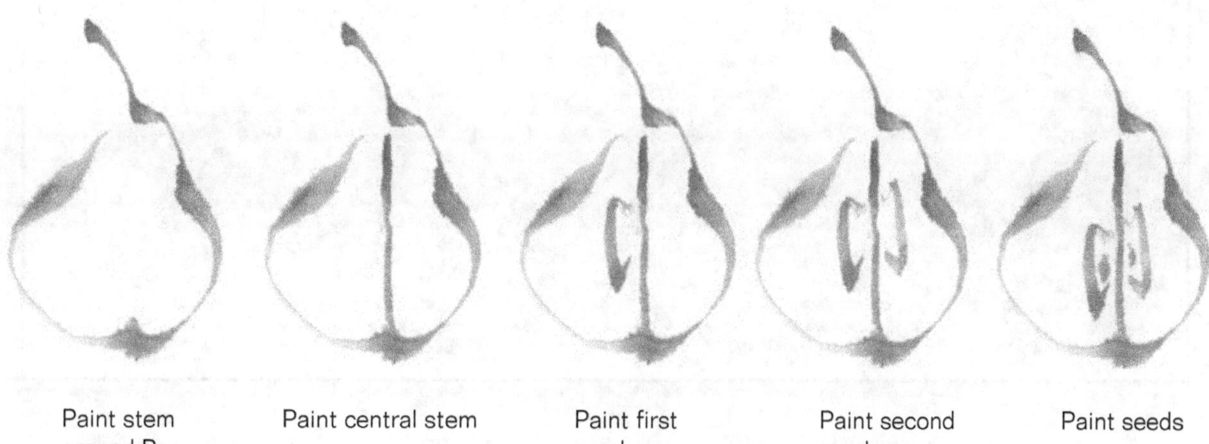

| Paint stem around Pear | Paint central stem | Paint first seed area | Paint second seed area | Paint seeds |

Leaf

The leaf is painted as a Horizon brushstroke, beginning at the tip of the stem and flowing with one or two curves, before lifting off with a point.

Veins can also be added as described in Plum Blossom.

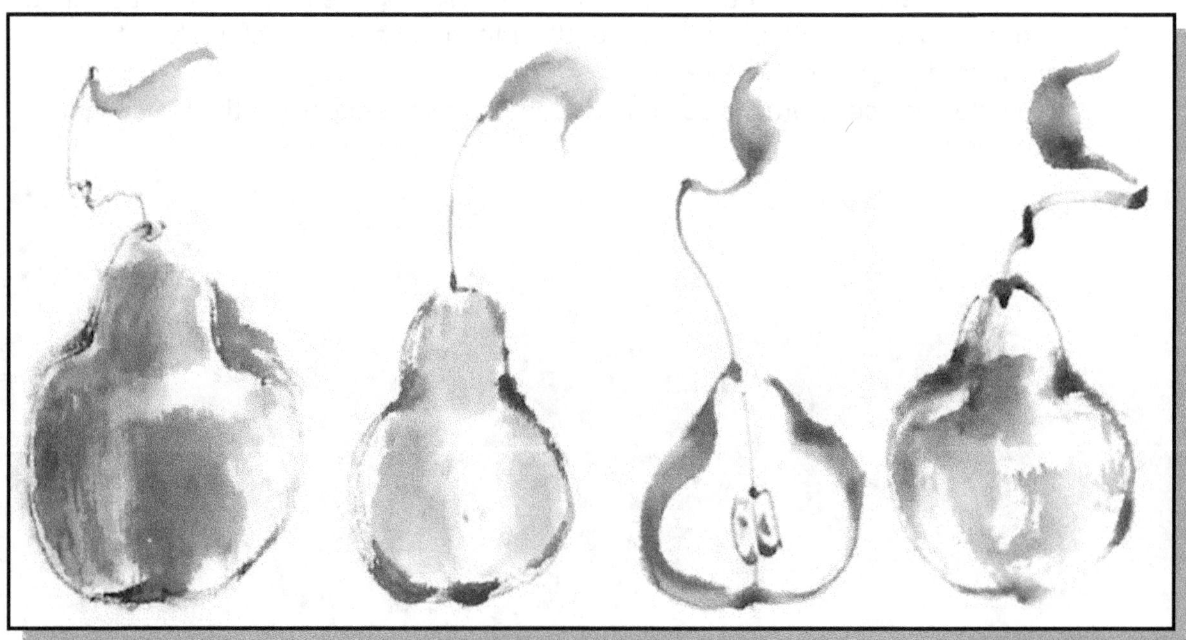

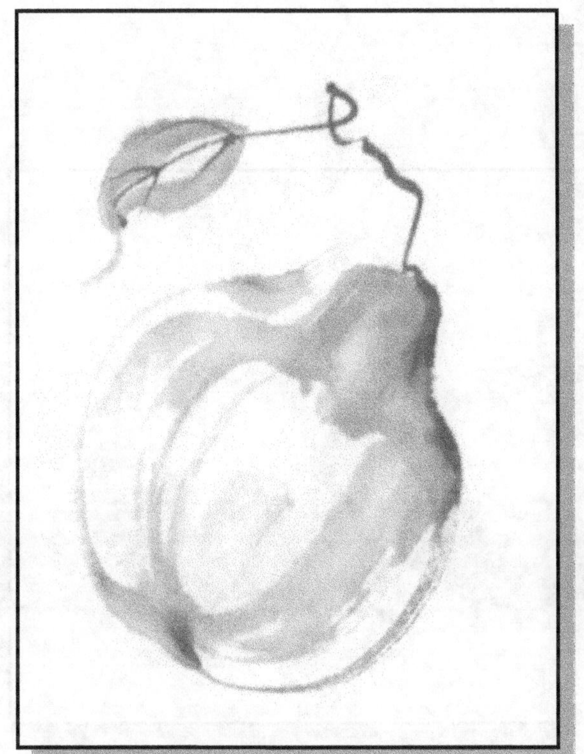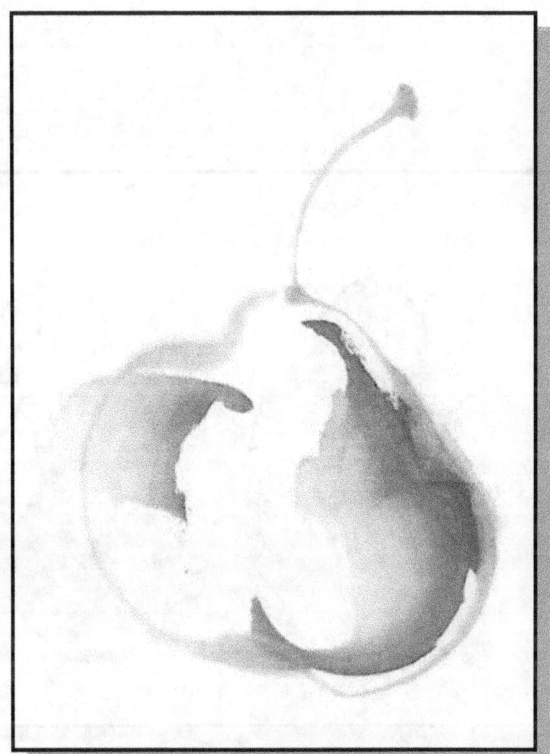

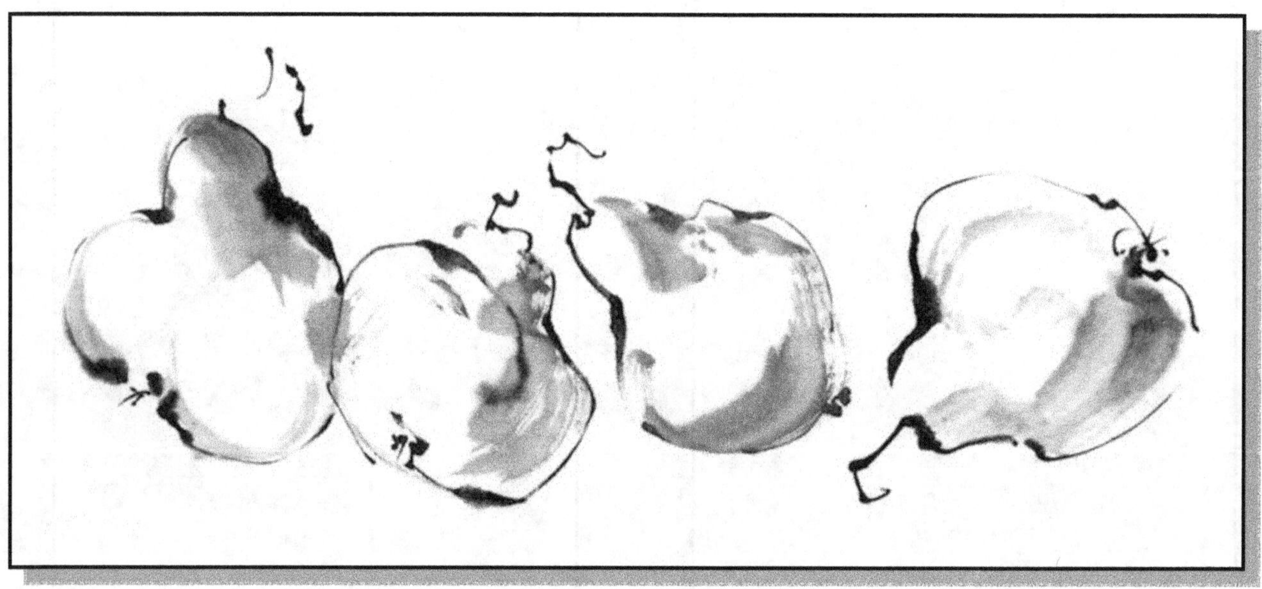

Wild Orchid
Spring — A Symbol of Grace, Love, Quiet Beauty, Elegance and Refinement

The Grass Orchid, Wind Orchid or Samurai Orchid is a joyous flower to paint. Its leaves extend out in invitation. The flower almost smiles for the artist's brush. Painting this subject will help the artist understand the balance of line and white space (yohaku). This simple form is one of the most difficult to master, yet it is one of the best examples of using the flowing lines so often present in sumi-e.

The Flower

The flower petals are delicate and gentle with a feeling of joyous dance.

Before beginning the flower head, one can place a dot of water on the page to indicate the base or centre of the flower. You will paint the petal brushstrokes toward this point without actually reaching it.

The wild orchid has five petals. The petals are all painted together while envisioning not each individual petal, but all the petals forming an embrace. The petals are painted from the outer tip toward the centre (the small dot of water). Each petal is painted generally in the following manner:

1. Bring the brush-tip down to the paper while breathing out.
2. As soon as the brush touches the paper, slow down a bit while still moving in a gentle curve, allowing the moisture to slip from brush to paper, giving a softly rounded tip to the petal.
3. Apply a bit more pressure accompanied by a nodding down of your head and, if you are standing, a bending of your knees while the brush continues to move through the curve of the stroke.
4. Continue your gentle movement while lifting the brush — raise your head and straighten your knees — not stopping until the brush has left the paper.

The short petals are painted with just a small breath out for each, and the brush gently coming down to touch the paper and, after a small petal stroke, gently rising until the brush is no longer on the paper.

Within this petal embrace are three anthers (the part of the stamen that has the pollen). They are Dots with "attitude," painted rhythmically and close together. Three puffs of air help create these saucy dots of ink, allowing a hair-width trailing of ink to indicate the direction the brush is moving in next. Use the Dot brushstroke that looks like a little bird and treat the set of dots as a dance, so they will indeed have attitude!

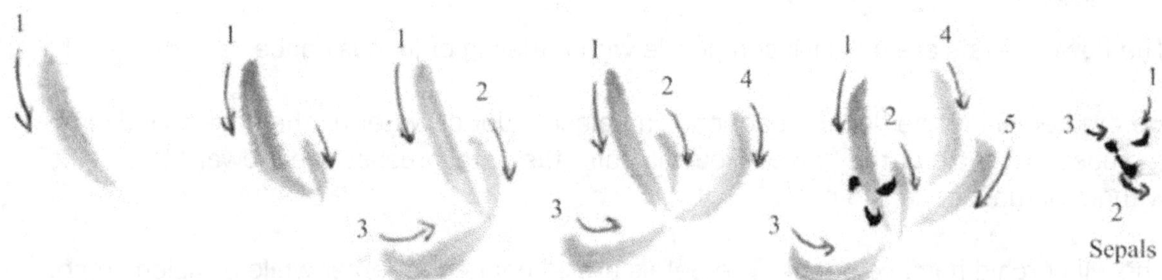

Paint flowers from the tips in. The 3 sepals are painted with rhythm and attitude!

The Stem

The stem can either be painted as one long, strong Bone stroke, with a natural curve, painted in one long breath, or as a series of overlapping bone brushstrokes.
In both cases, the stem also forms a gradual curve from flower head to the ground.

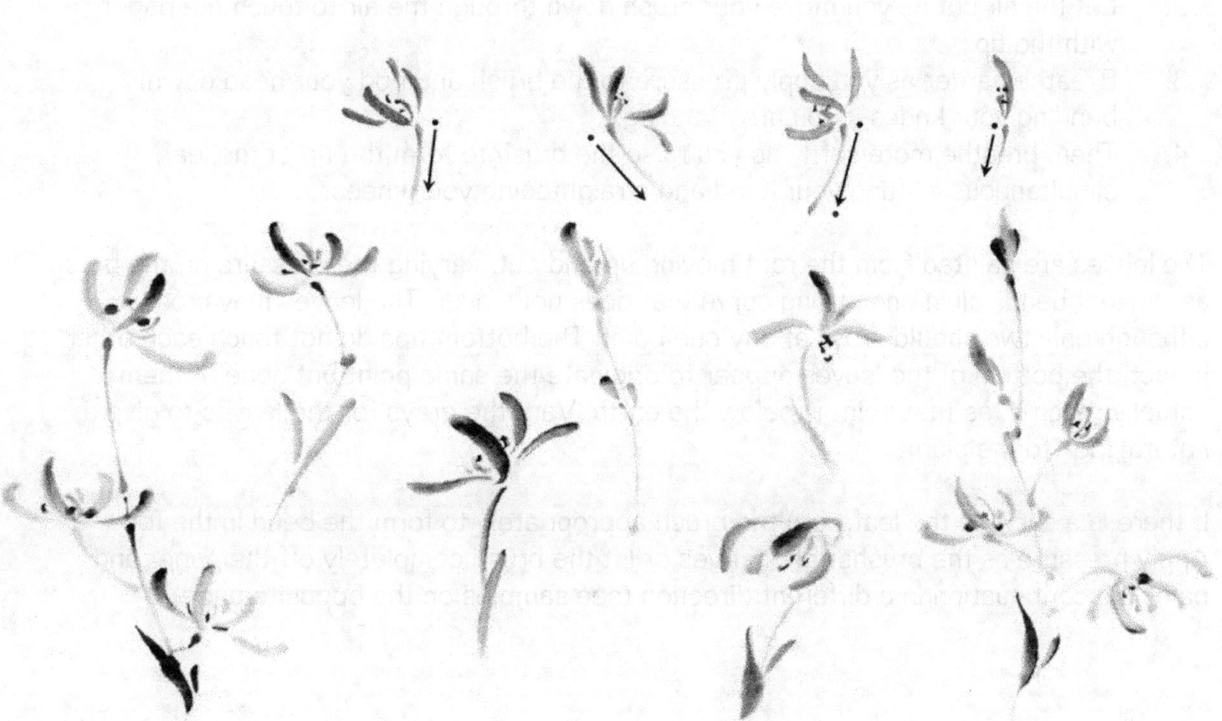

The Leaves

The leaves of this plant are strong, supple and elegant, almost like the limbs of a dancer. These strokes are painted with a spontaneous and free-flowing feeling.

1. Begin with the brush in the air, and with an intake of breath.
2. Let the air out as you move your brush down through the air to touch the paper with the tip.
3. Breathe harder as you apply pressure to the brush and nod your head down, bending your knees if you are standing.
4. Then, breathe more softly as you raise the brush to form the tip of the leaf, simultaneously lifting your head and straightening your knees.

The leaves are painted from the root moving up and out, varying the pressure on the brush as the leaf bends all in one strong curve that does not waver. The leaves may cross, although only two should cross at any one point. The bottom tips do not touch each other. In fact, the bottom of the leaves appear to originate the same point but none of them actually reach it, as that point is below the earth. Vary the grays for the leaves to give a natural look to the plant.

If there is a curve in the leaf, turn the brush appropriately to form the bend in the form. Apply pressure as the brushstroke curves or lift the brush completely off the paper and paint the continuation in a different direction (see samples on the opposite page).

For the leaves, work from the earth and upward.
Feel their stiffness yet flexibility

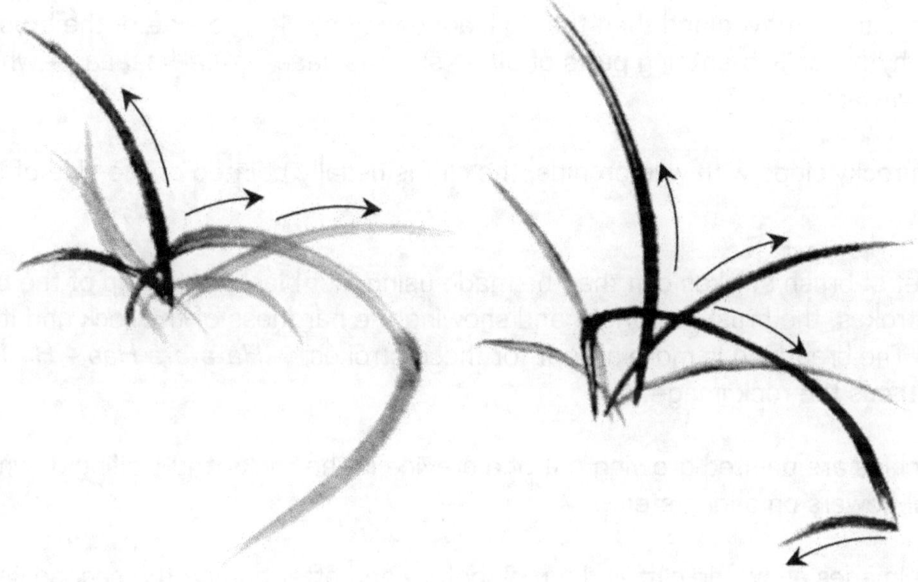

The Feeling of Rocky Cliff

These flowers can be painted as growing out of the ground or out of the side of a cliff.

Rocky cliffs are painted with strong stokes accompanied by rhythmic out-puffs of air, with the length of the stoke and pressure used reflected in the amount of air expelled — as always, with a nodding of the head and bending of the knees. The strokes used are a combination of Bone and Horizon brushstrokes, using the side of the brush — by which I mean that you may enter the stroke as a Horizon stroke, continuing with rhythmic Bone strokes, and ending softly as a Horizon brushstroke.

The first set of rock strokes are done with the brush loaded with a lighter colour gray ink; some of the liquid removed and then the tip loaded with black. The side of the brush is used while rhythmically breathing puffs of air — such as *haaa-ha-ha-haaaaa* — while painting downward.

If painting a rocky slope with wild orchids, the cliff is usually painted at the side of the paper.

A second set of brush strokes can then be made using just black on the tip of the brush. For these strokes, the brush is upright and showing the hardness of the rock and its cragginess. The breathing is more abrupt for these strokes — *Ha-a-a-a Haa – Ha-Ha Ha!* This strengthens the rock image.

The wild orchids are painted growing out of a crevice in the rocks and trailing downward, with several flowers on a long stem.

The sample images show the cliff and a rock before and after adding the second set of brushstrokes.

Feel the sharpness and hardness of the rocks while painting them.

Note that the spacing between the puffs of air is not even, which makes for a more natural shape.

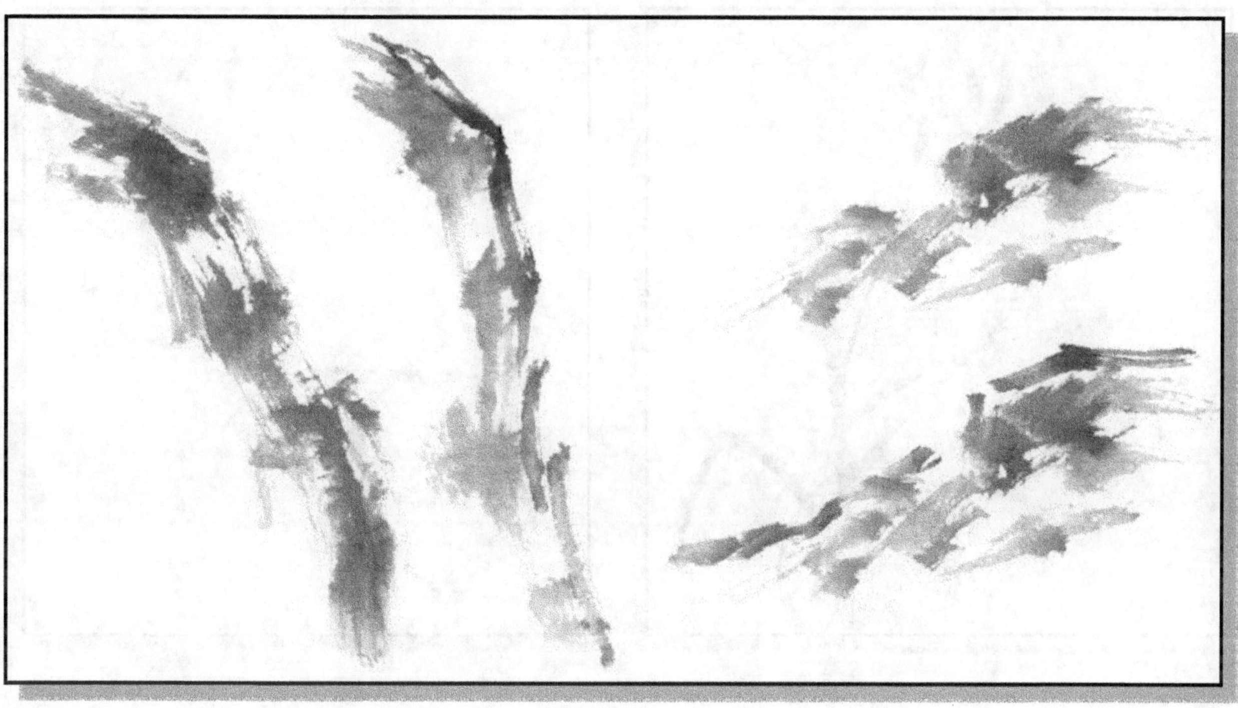

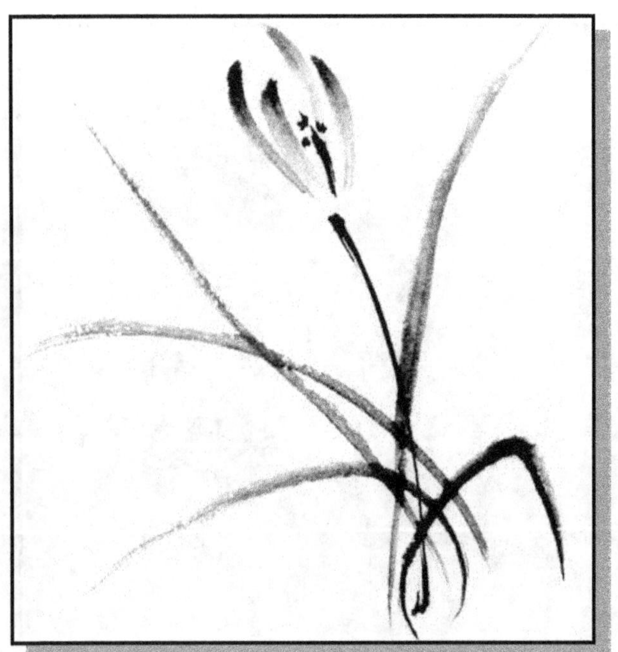 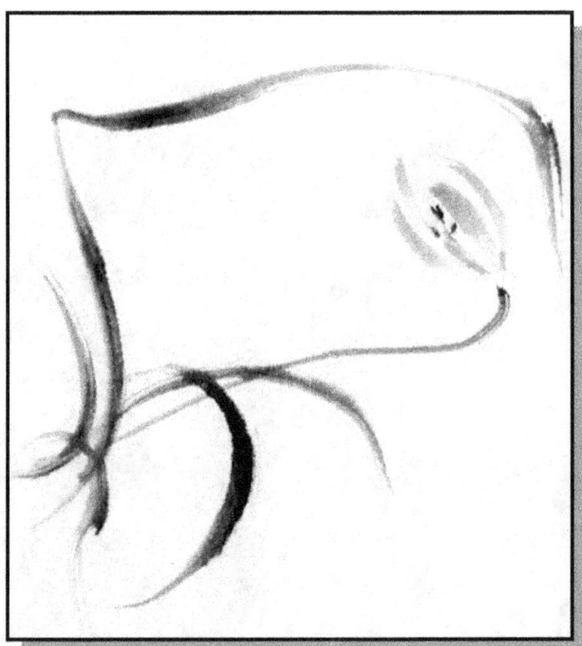

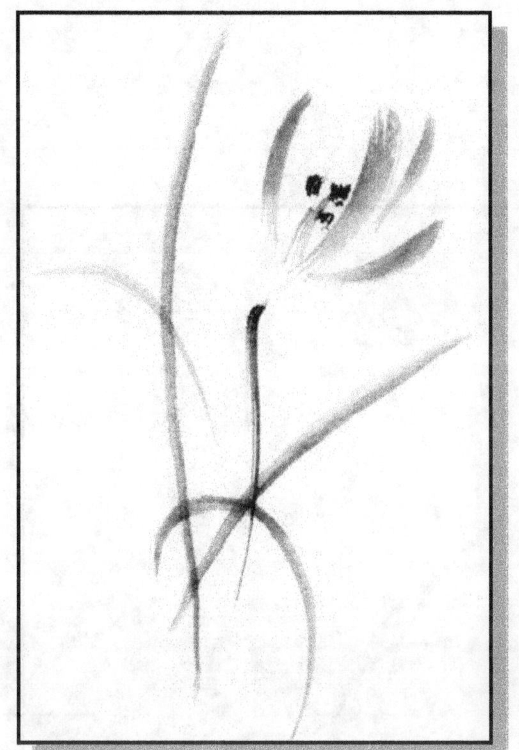

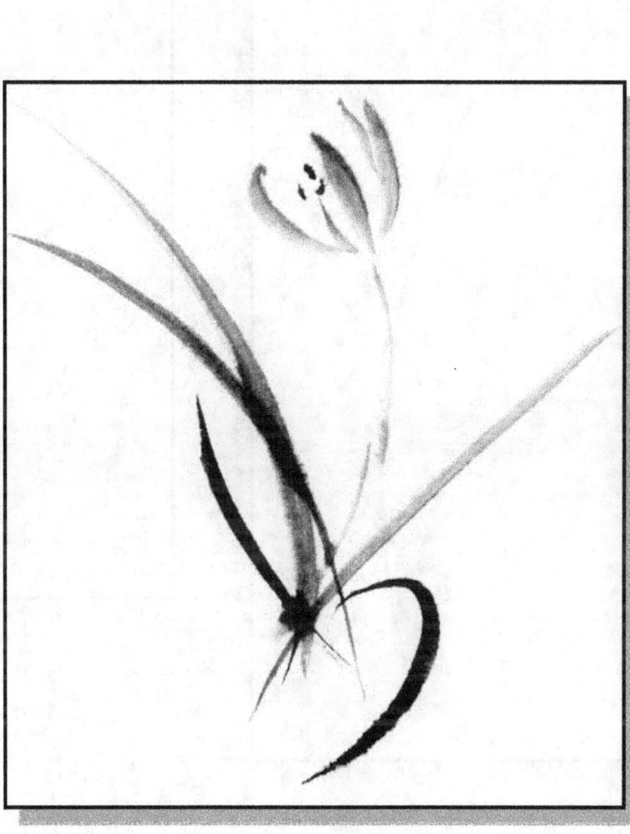

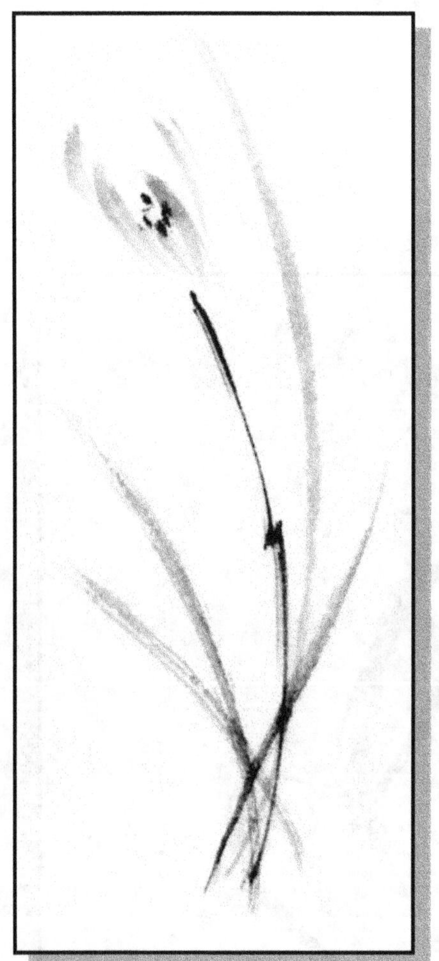

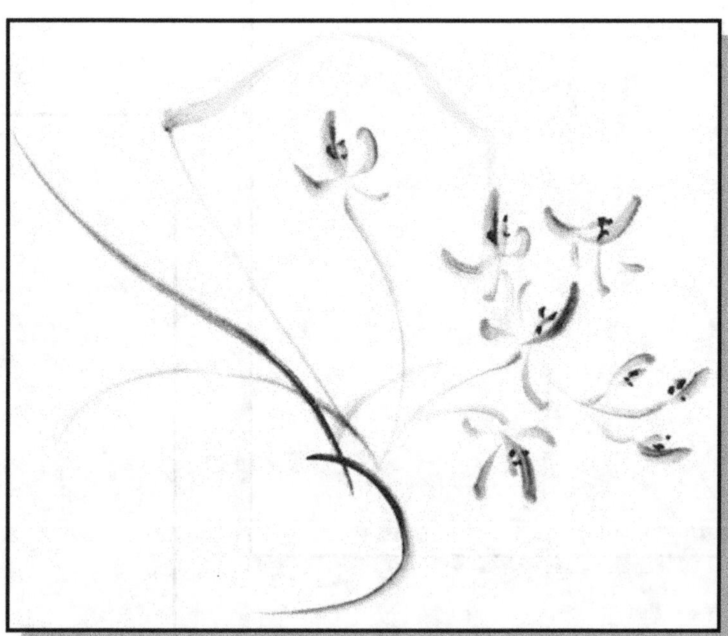

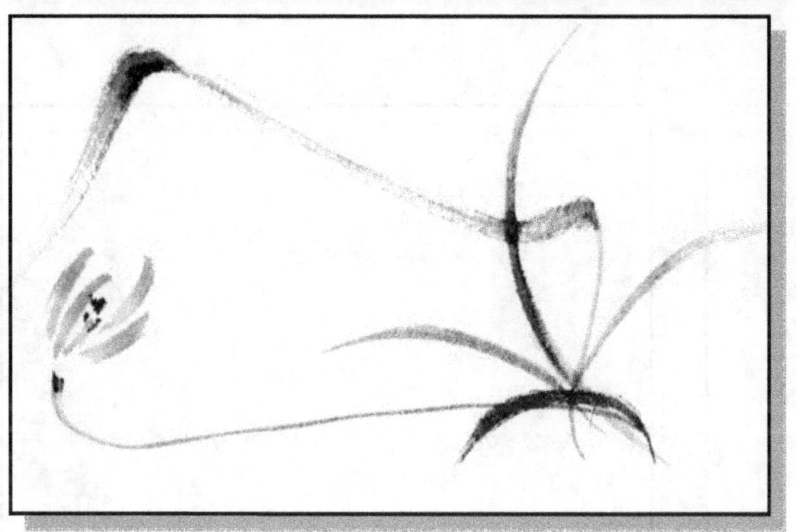

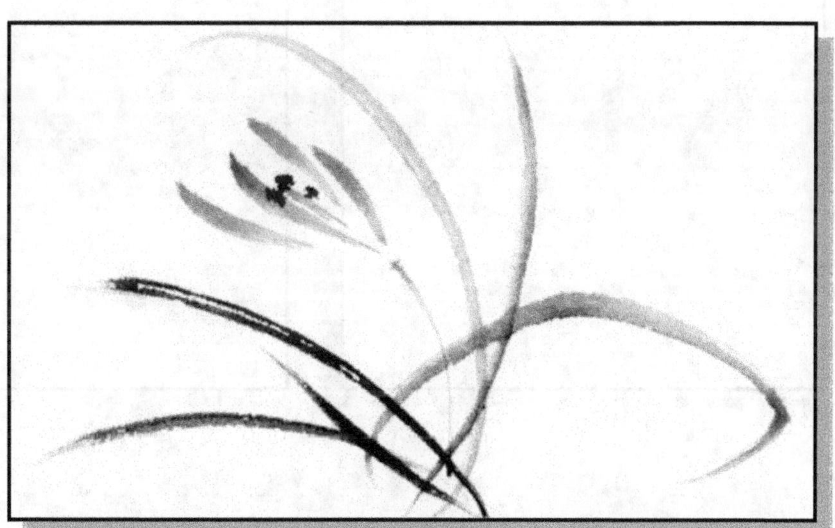

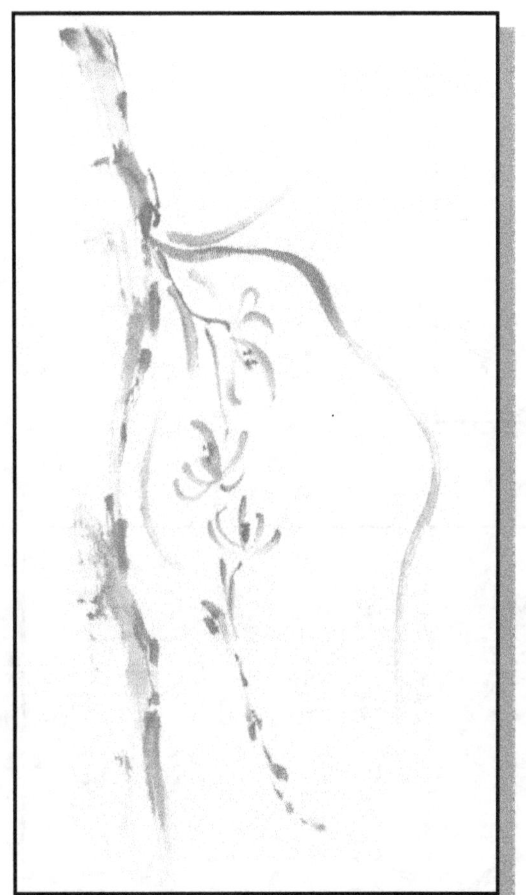 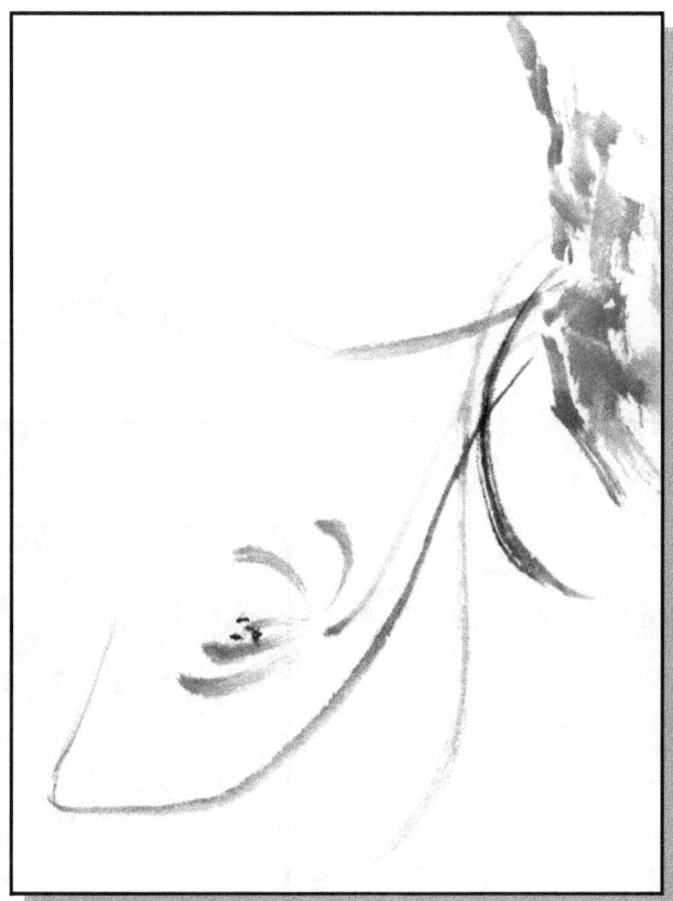

Chrysanthemum
Autumn — Symbol of Integrity, Friendship and Joviality

The flower of the chrysanthemum can be painted in two manners, using either one or two brushstrokes for each petal.

Flower Using One Brushstroke Per Petal

1. The petals of this flower all originate form a disk-shape at the centre or heart of the flower. Begin by placing a drop of water at the centre of the heart of the flower head. Your petals will aim for this centre point but will rarely reach it.

2. Begin painting the petals at the centre of the flower with darker ink. These petals are the smallest. All the petals are painted from the ends toward the centre. These first petals are painted as a group of seven. The first three petals begin at the centre and go on a slant upwards. Next a set of four beginning just beside the first of the previous three and slanting upwards in the other direction. These brushstrokes are painted with rhythmic puffs of breath, such as *pah-pah-pah-pahpah-pah-pah*. Together the base of the petals should form a lopsided 'V.' For each of these petals the brush is upright. Inhale. When the brush touches the paper, expel a '*pah*' and continue expelling your breath while moving and lift the brush, curving toward the centre, keeping each petal quite short yet lively. Remember these are the shortest petals.

3. The second layer of petals are longer. They are like fingers gathering sunshine around the flower in a few rows. Paint a few on one side and a few on the other, shifting from side to side. Begin at the tip of each petal and curve toward the centre, as you did for the centre petals, except these are longer. Also paint a few partial petals that are on the opposite side of the flower, remembering to leave a bit of space for the stamens. Use rhythm and flow to allow for a natural curve for each petal. The petals should not crowd each other, but they should feel like they are all part of the same flower head.

4. After one to several layers of these petals, begin the final row of petals. These are different in that some of them will curve upward and some downward. They are

sparser and longer than the second layer of petals for the most part, varying in length, yet painted in the same manner. Keep your brushstrokes firm and lively — natural!

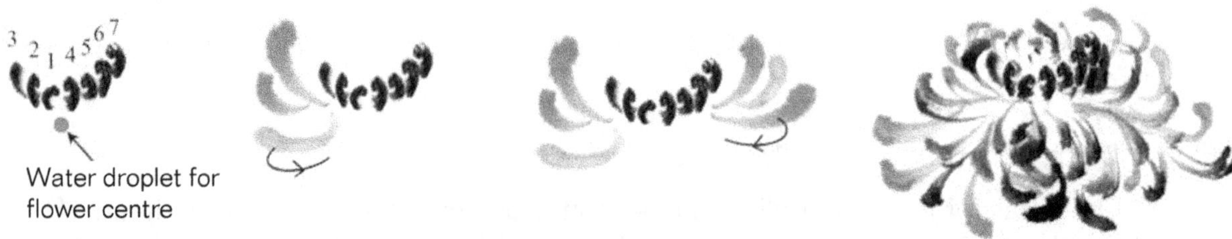

Flower Using Two Brushstrokes Per Petal

Flowers using two brushstrokes per petal are shaped like open umbrellas with the uppermost central portion having the stamens in it.

1. Begin by painting the stamens as several firm individual dots in black. These dots can look a bit rough and asymmetrical, not forming a circle, so they appear natural. **NOTE:** these stamens are not always visible. It depends upon the "pose" of the flower. You will see both instances in the sample images.
2. Load the brush with both a dark and lighter shade of gray.
3. Keep the brush upright and inhale.
4. Beginning at the centre of the flower with the Horizon stroke, paint the brushstroke using a downward and inward curve with a short hook at the end.
5. Paint the other side of the petal in the same manner but curved up toward the end of the hook. Do not match top and bottom of each petal precisely or the petals will not look natural.
6. Continue painting petals around the stamen centre, gradually shortening the petals as you get to the shortest ones at the back of the flower, varying the shades of gray on your brush.
7. Paint partial petals between the ones closest to the centre, only painting a few at the back of the flower.

8.   If the flower head is facing away, you will have to paint a calyx of four little leaves in darker ink — short Horizon strokes, painted quickly and rhythmically on the out breath, with the brush upright.

9.   For buds, paint a small number of petals, all upright, with the calyx at the base.

10.   For a partially opened flower, if the flower is partially facing you, just paint one row of petals with the central stamens painted first. If it is totally upright or facing away, paint the calyx at its base.

11.   **Always be aware that the flowers must look natural and relaxed.**

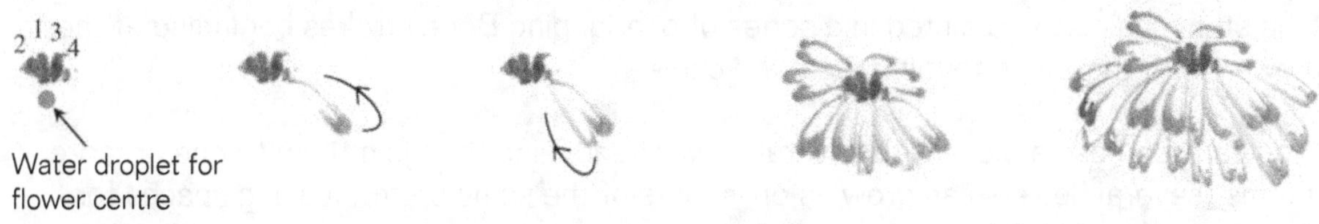

Flower Bud

The bud is just a few of the first petals all curling around their centre, as if for protection.

Around the grouping of petals at the base of the flower are the sepals. They are short Horizon strokes in black, usually three or five, all painted from the tip to the bottom centre of the flower head, pointed at each end.

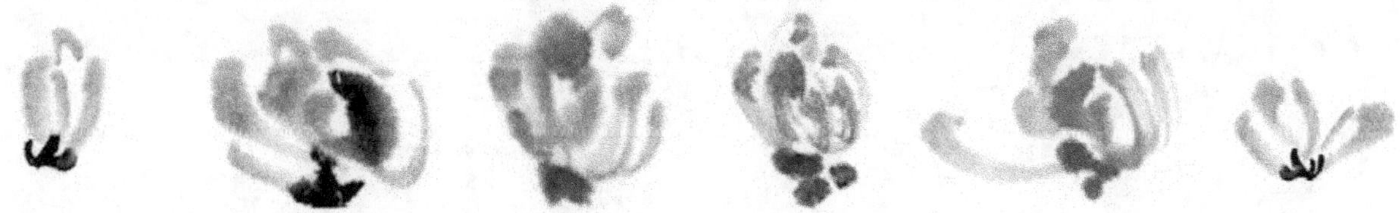

Stem

Begin at the base of the flower and paint a long, firm, naturally curved Bone stroke, sometimes leaving a little space for a leaf to cut across the stem.

If the stem is from a secondary flower, end its stem at the main stem.
Sometimes the stem has little hairs on it. These are painted with the tip of the brush, using tiny Horizon brushstrokes. Make certain you do not try to always end the hairs right on the side of the stem, as that will not look natural. Just keep moving and placing the brushstrokes randomly about the stem.

The stem can also be painted in a series of overlapping Bone strokes beginning at the flower, with the whole forming a natural curve.

You can compose a piece with several flower heads and then join them to one or more stems (several flowers can grow as off-shoots of the same stem), leaving spaces for leaves.

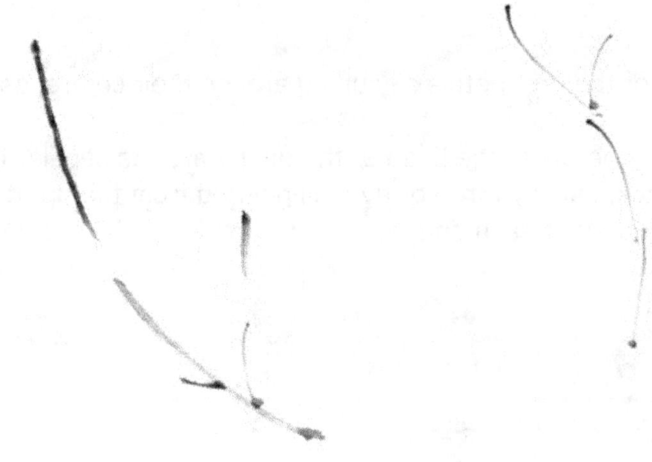

Leaves

On this plant there are little, immature leaves at points on the stem near the flower head. For each of these leaves, hold the brush upright and inhale. While exhaling, bring the brush to the paper with a puff of breath, then curve the stroke down and inwards to touch the stem. These leaves are very short.

For the other leaves:

1. Load the brush with two shades of gray.
2. Using the side of the brush, paint a central longer Horizon stroke and a shorter one on either side, touching the centre stroke, all slightly curved on the same trajectory.
3. While the three strokes are still damp, paint the veins with darker ink, using the Horizon brushstroke. In each of the three parts of the leaf there is a central stem, and a few veins going off the main vein that are offset from each other. These brushstrokes curve toward the edge of the leaf, following its natural shape, but they do not necessarily touch the edge of the leaf; however, they can go past the edge of the leaf.
4. The leaves can also be made more complex with more than three lobes, or more side lobes on one side.
5. They can also be shown from the side with an extra brushstroke curving the tip naturally into a point, and the closer side a lighter gray than the farther side, or visa versa.

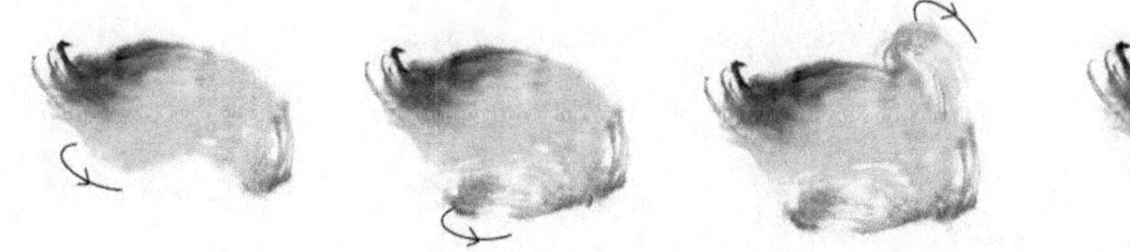
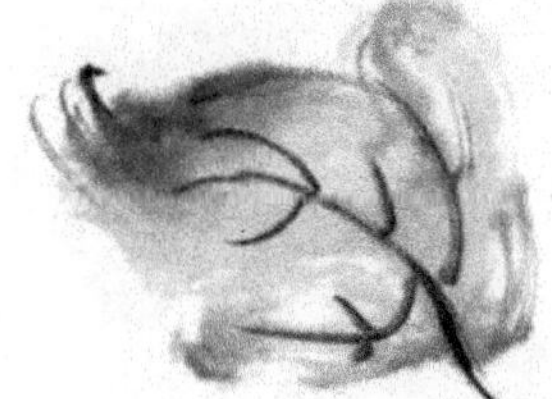

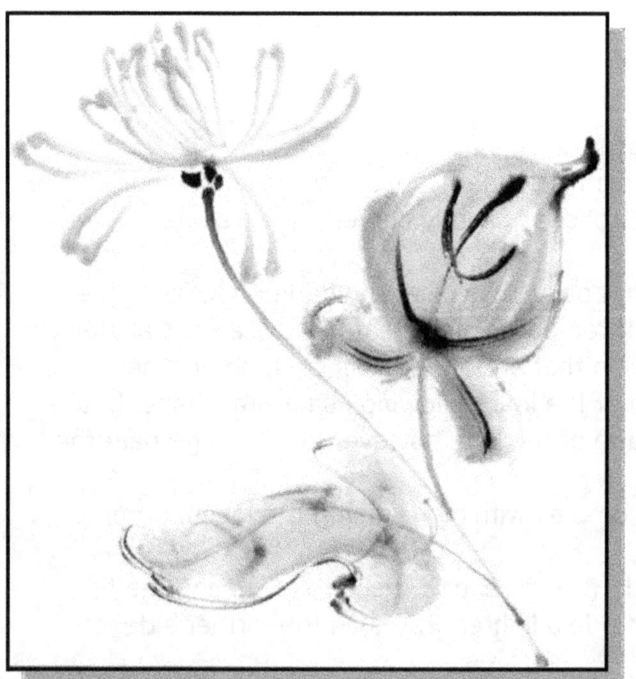 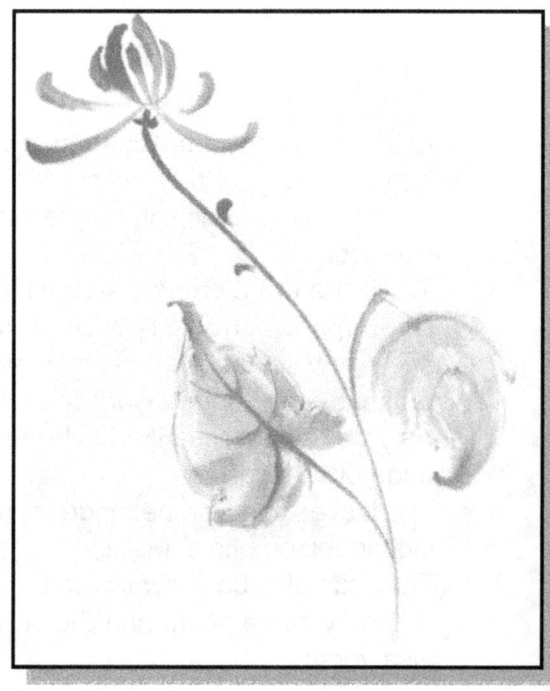

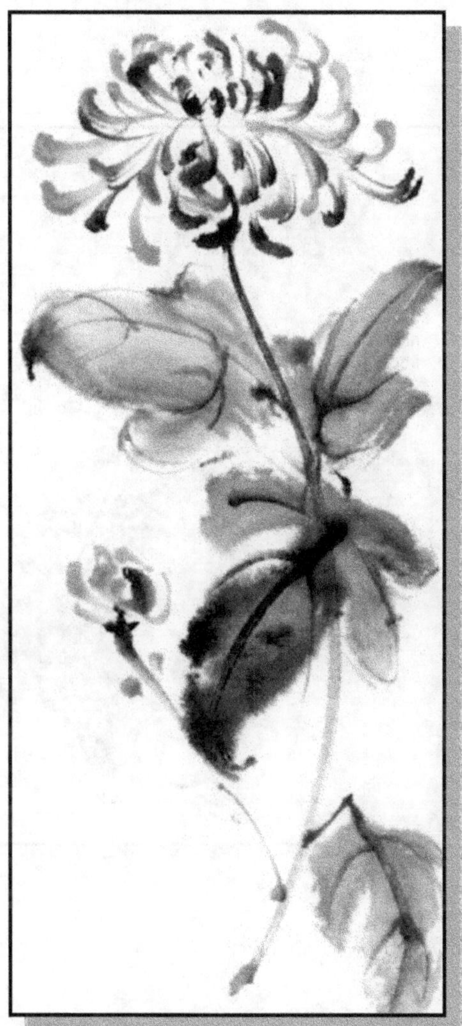
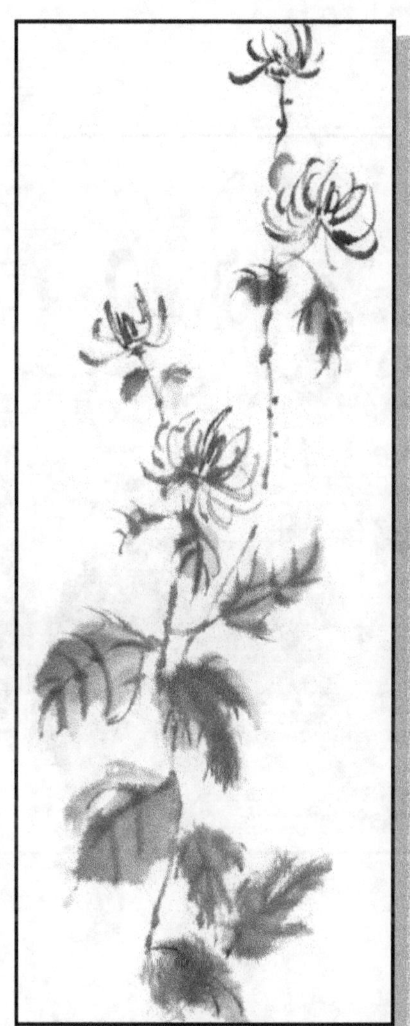

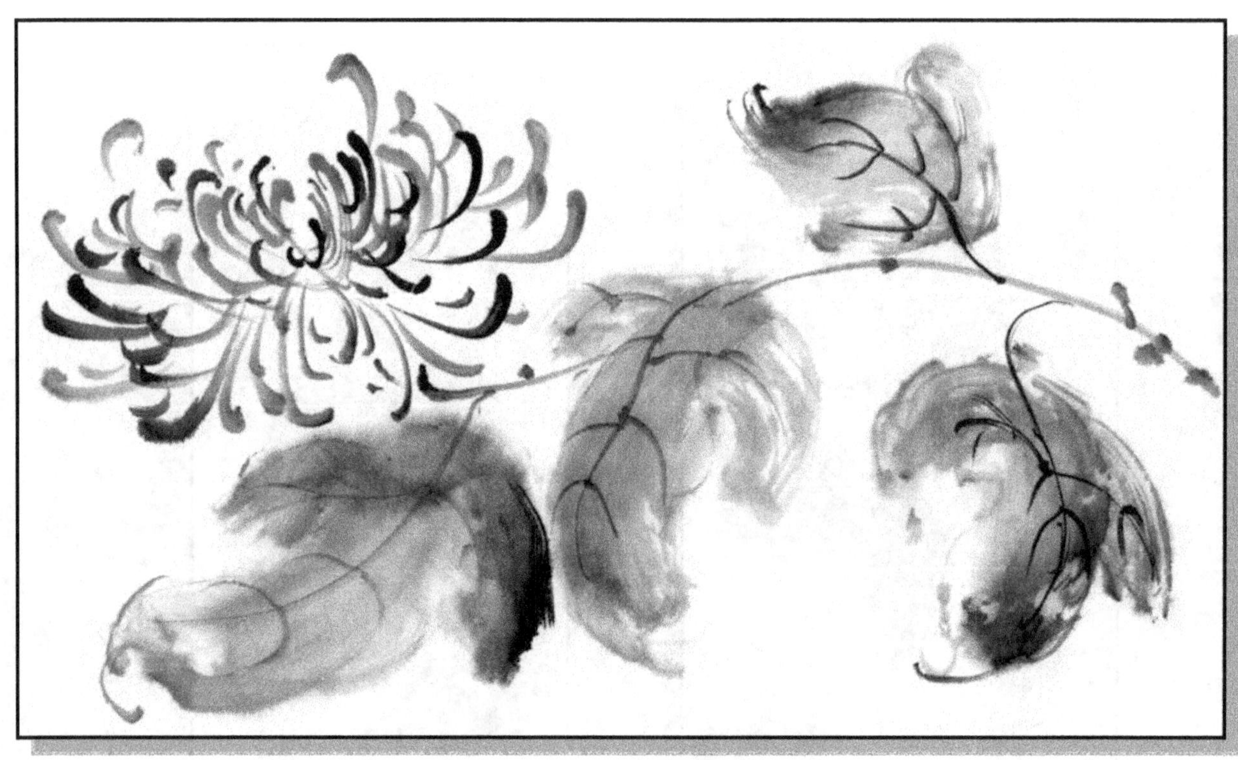

Plum Blossom
Winter — Symbol of Purity, Strength, Courage and Perseverance

Plum blossom flowers can either be painted "boneless" (without outline) or with each petal outlined. The flowers of the plum blossom have five petals surrounding several stamens, with a spray of dots above them. The manner in which you paint the stamens will determine the direction the flower is facing.

Petals in Both Methods

Each petal is painted using the Horizon brushstroke following the shape below — the tail at the beginning being the path followed by the brush at the start of the exhale, while in the air. As soon as the brush touches the paper, change direction and create a petal.

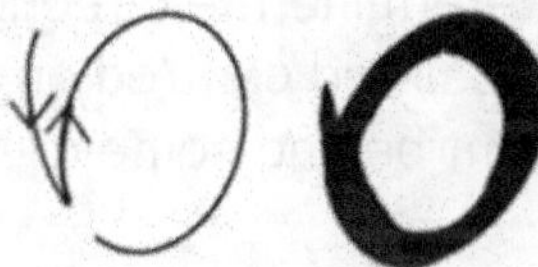

In the Outline Method

1. Apply pressure so the petals are circumscribed rather than solid.
2. Sometimes a stop can occur at one end, as is done for the Bone stroke.
3. Each circle should be imperfect and natural.
4. Each flower has five petals, but not all petals can always be seen, so they need not all be painted for each flower.
5. Inhale and paint several sets of petals to form a composition of flowers.
6. Remember that you are not painting individual petals but, rather, a flower consisting of several individual petals.

In the **Boneless Method**, apply more pressure so that the petals are solid when completed; otherwise, follow the instructions for the Outline Method.

Buds

Whether painting the flowers in either method, the bud is one or two petals with three small dark leaves at the bottom and a stem.

Boneless Method   Outline Method

Stamens

The way you paint the stamens will determine the direction the flower is facing. For a flower facing the viewer, they can be painted centred on the middle of the petals in a circle, or they can be centred on a point behind some of the petals, pointing in any direction painted in a partial circle.

- Using the Horizon brushstroke, with the brush upright, move the arm holding the brush back and forth, barely touching the paper with the tip.
- Note that the brush will not always touch the paper as you go back and forth painting stamens. That is okay.
- After painting what appears to be a sufficient number of stamens, use the tip of the brush to place small dots about the tips of the stamens.
- All must be done in a natural manner. That means that you do not aim for the tip of each stamen to place a dot. Be random and natural.

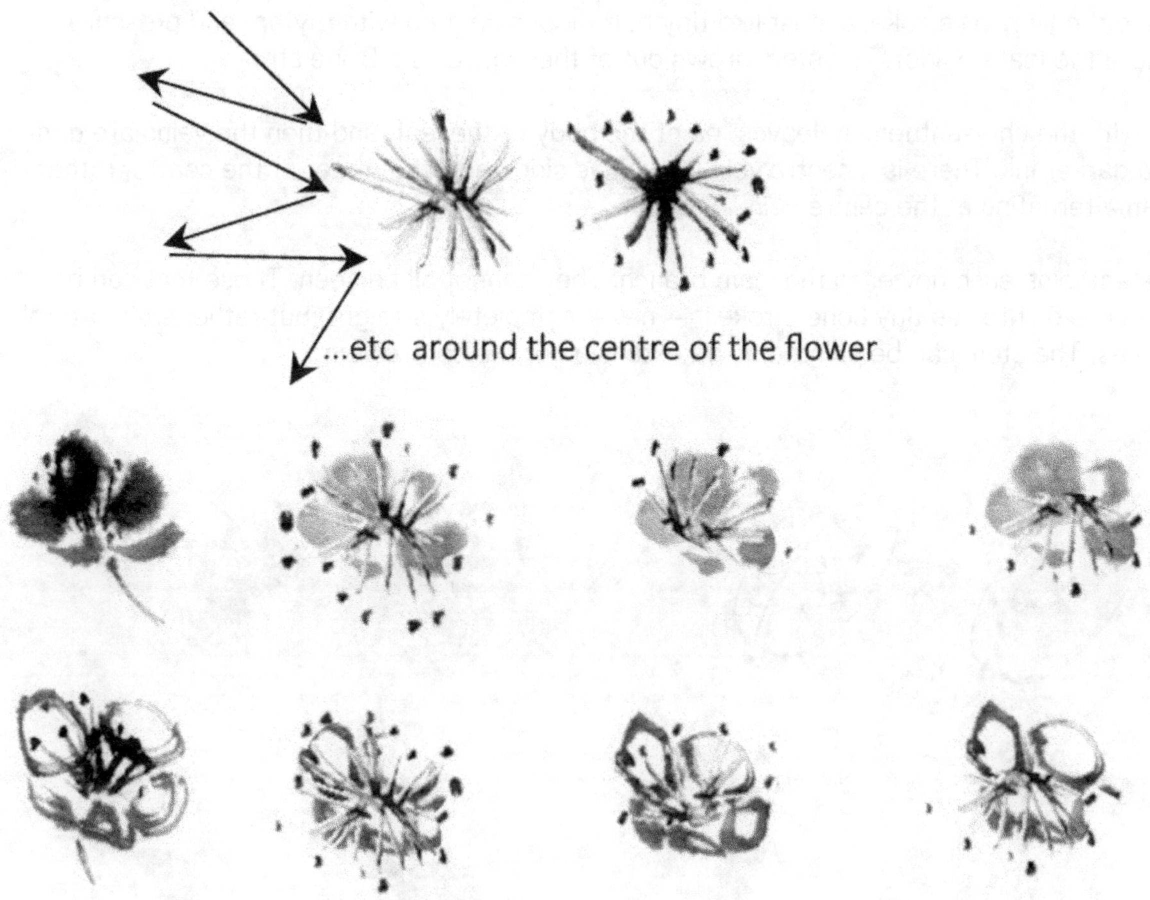
...etc around the centre of the flower

Leaves and Stems

If a flower is facing away or partially away from the viewer, there will be three small dark leaves around the bottom of the flower head around the stem. These are painted, again using the Horizon stroke, almost like tiny half-moons painted with rhythm and pressure where the leaf is wider. The stem grows out of the centre as a Bone stroke.

As with the chrysanthemum leaves, paint the body of the leaf, and then the veins are done in a darker ink. There is a centre vein as well as side veins that meet at the centre, rather than alternating at the centre vein.

A stem joins each flower to the main branch. They cannot all be seen. Those that can be seen are painted as tiny bone strokes — never completely straight, but rather with natural curves. The stem can be painted as an extension of the centre vein.

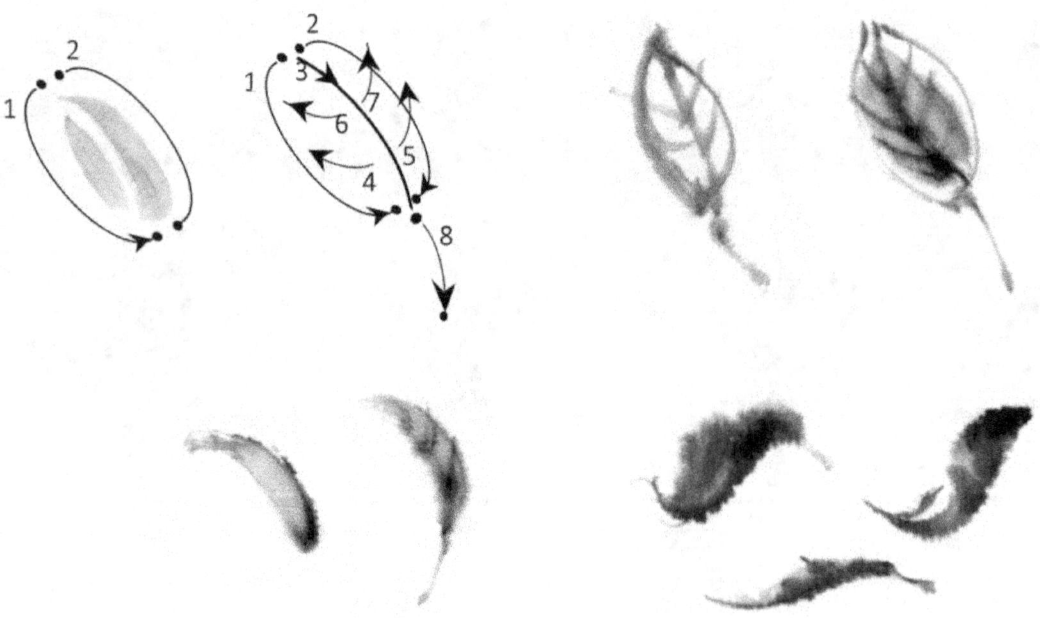

Branches

Look at the branches of any tree. They are larger at the trunk and become more and more slender toward the end. They are not straight. They curve gently although the last bit of each branch may be rather straight.

1. Use a drier brush with varied shades of gray on the brush to begin.
2. Use the Bone stroke until the very end of the branch where the brush is lifted as in the end of the Horizon brushstroke to give a soft, delicately pointed end.
3. One begins with more pressure on the brush tip, or using the side of the brush.
4. Gradually raise the brush until just the tip is on the paper as you move along the branch and finally off the washi.
5. The branch is painted — rhythmically — with a series of connected Bone strokes. Each of the sequential Bone strokes are of different lengths, using less pressure as you move towards the end of the branch.
6. To create a curve, each little Bone stroke is at a different angle than the previous one, which in totality bend in a gracious curve.
7. After the initial set of brushstrokes to create the branch, side branches can be added. Note that where a side branch joins another branch, the side branch is no thicker than the main branch and becomes thinner towards the tip.
8. To give more texture to the branch, another thinner and darker set of brushstrokes can be added on one or both sides of the original.
9. The end of the brush can be flattened by hand to have many painted hairs, which can be used to delicately paint curves around the branch giving further texture to the bark.
10. In the case of plum blossom, there are also black dots on the bark representing beginning flower and leaf buds.
11. Use breath, movement of the body, and sound — *pah-pah,pah pah-pah-pah*, etc. — while painting branches.
12. Feel within yourself the strength of the branch — its flexibility, its texture — as you paint!
13. The branches can be painted first with spaces left for flowers to be placed, or the flowers can be painted first with the branches fitted around and through them.

14.   Extra branches or flowers can always be added to create a pleasing composition.

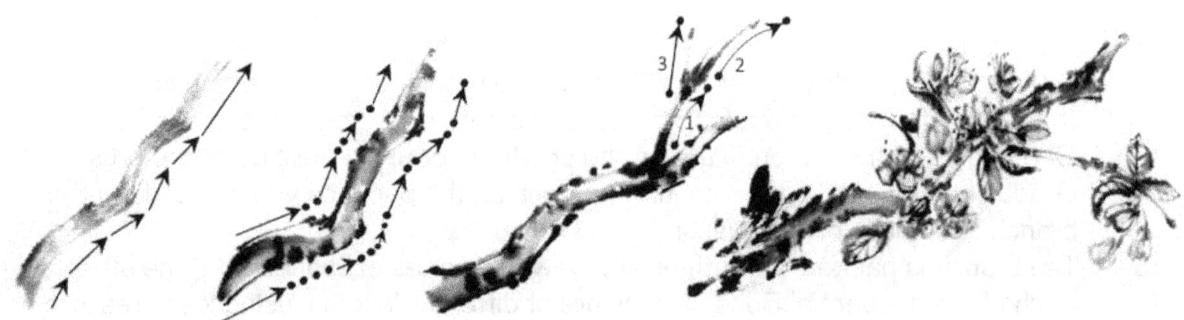

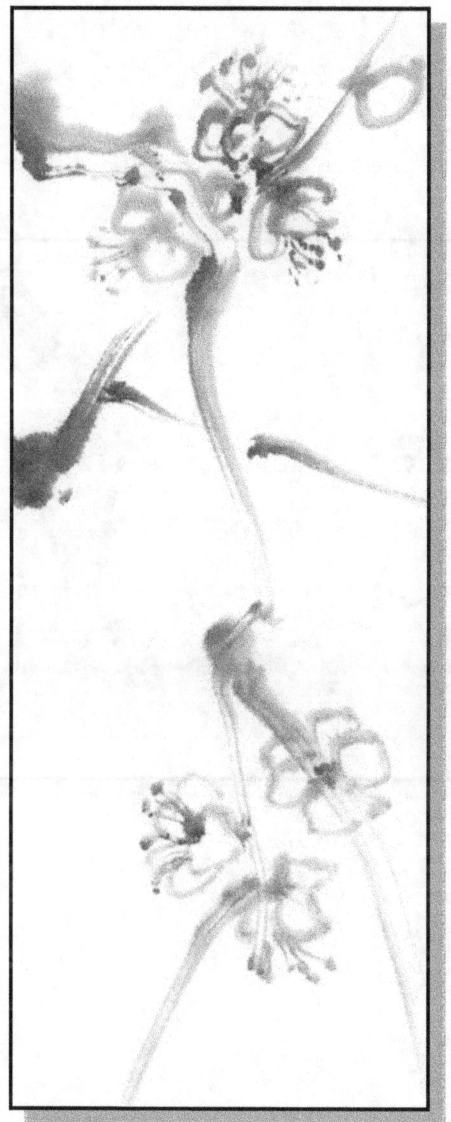 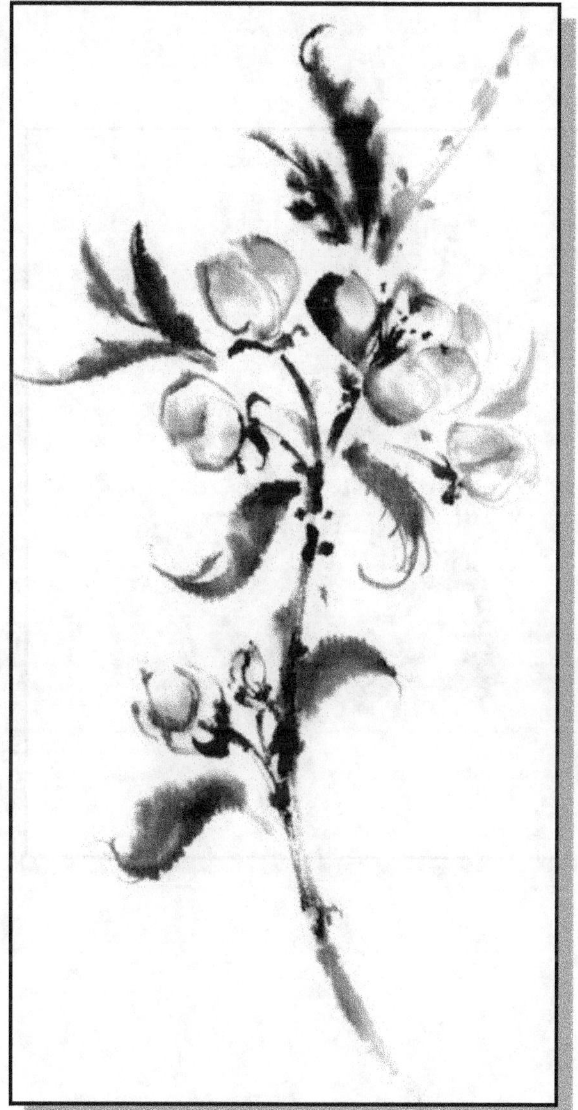

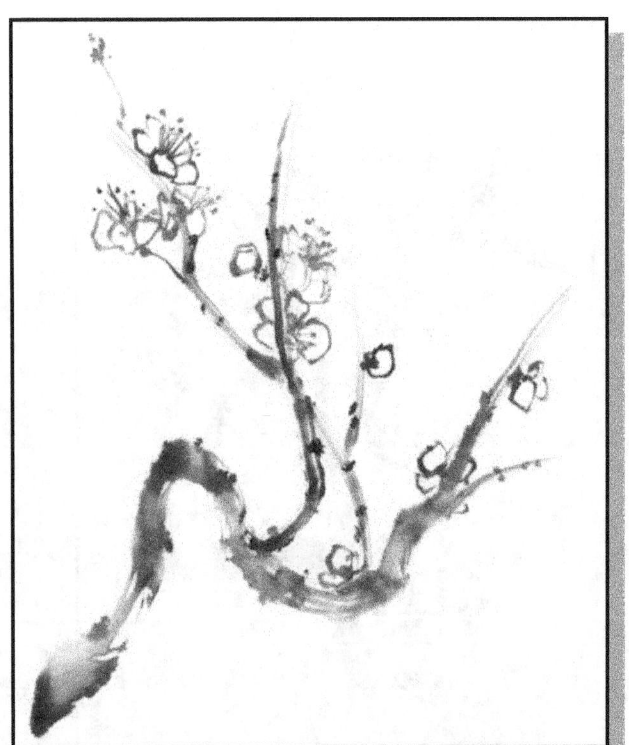

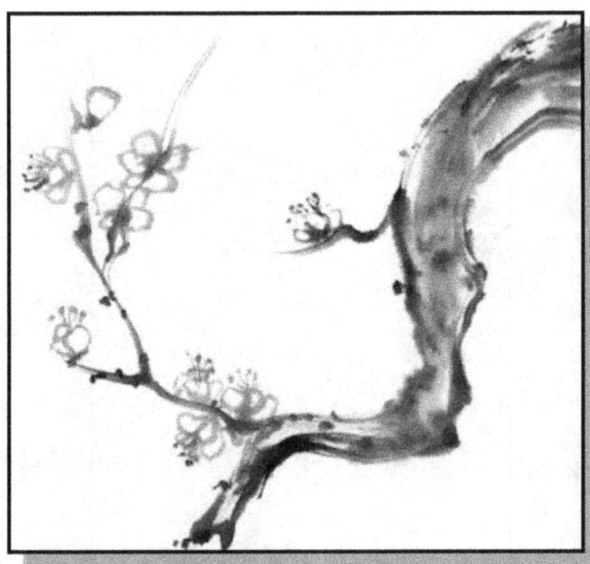

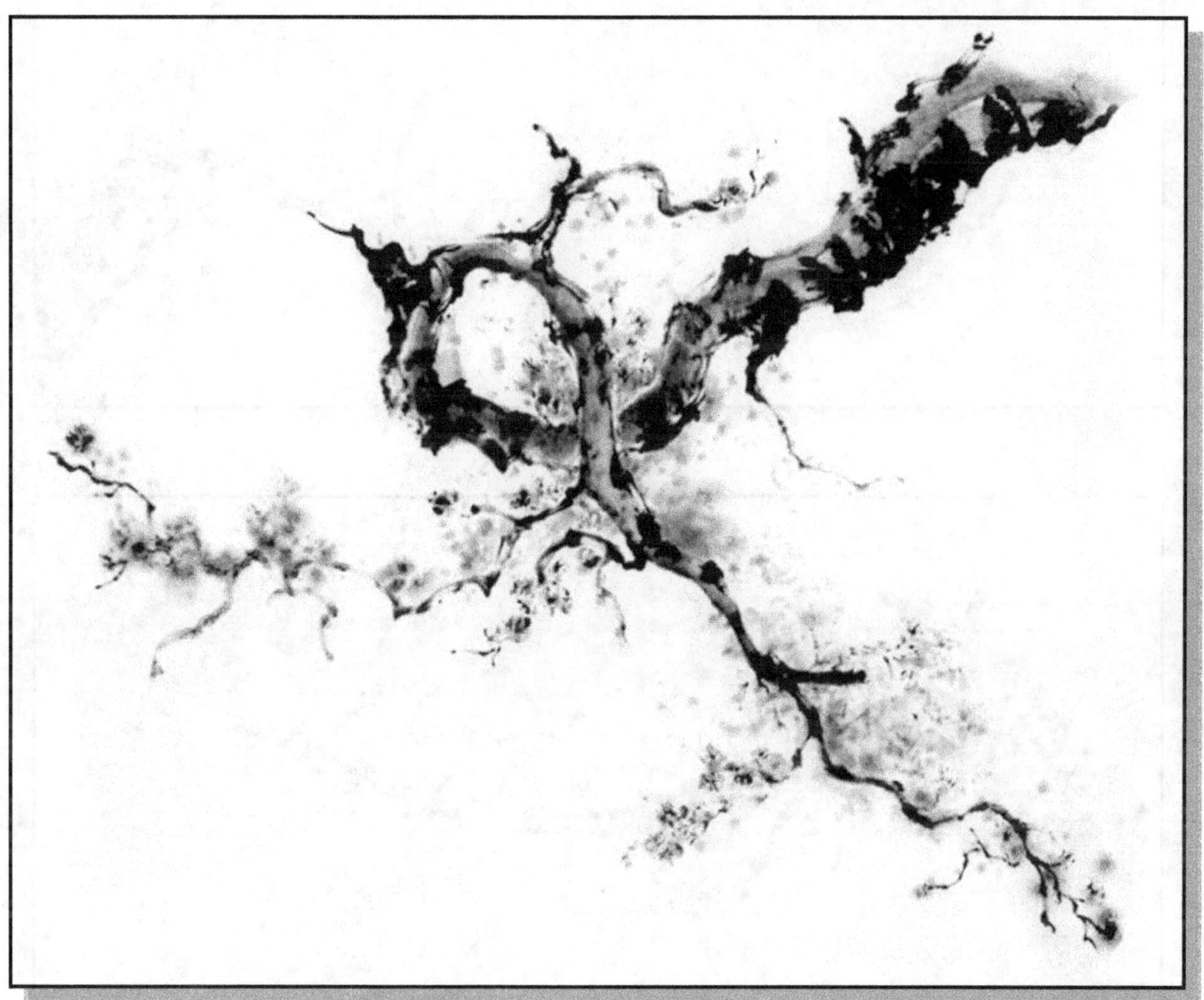

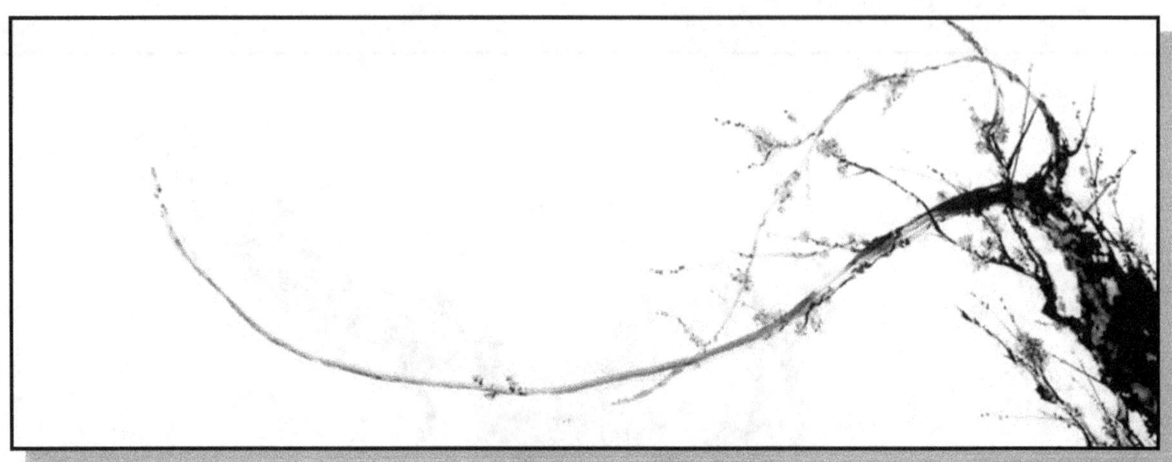

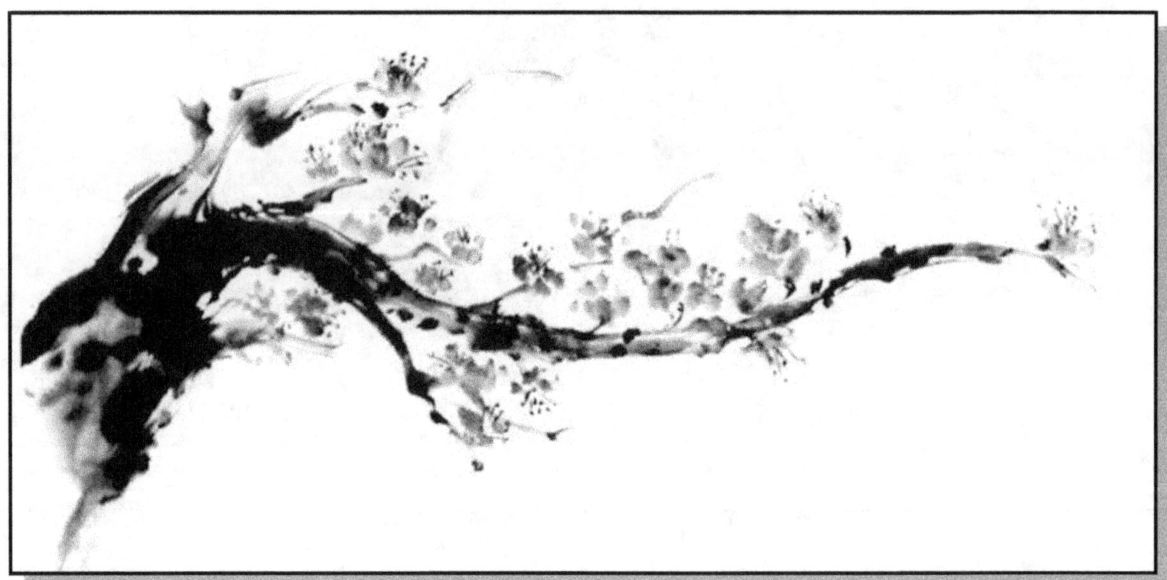

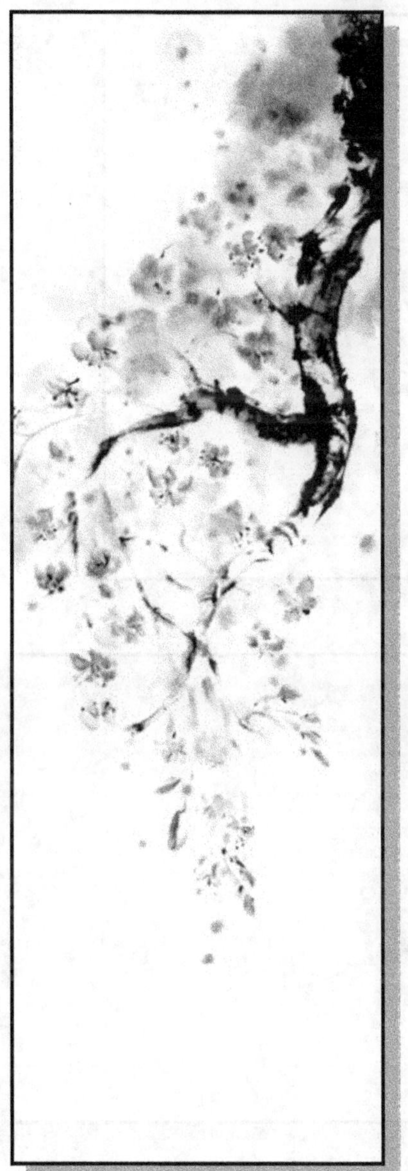

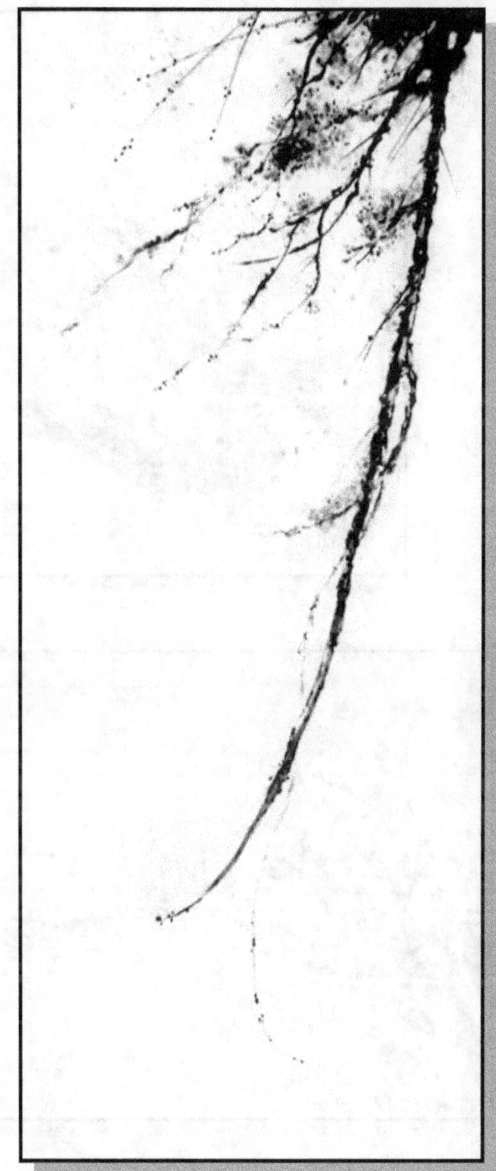

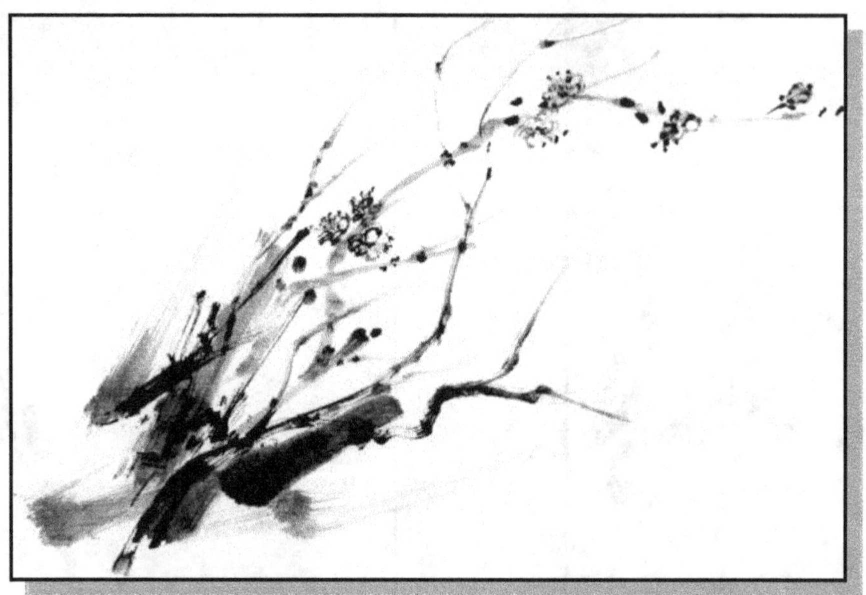

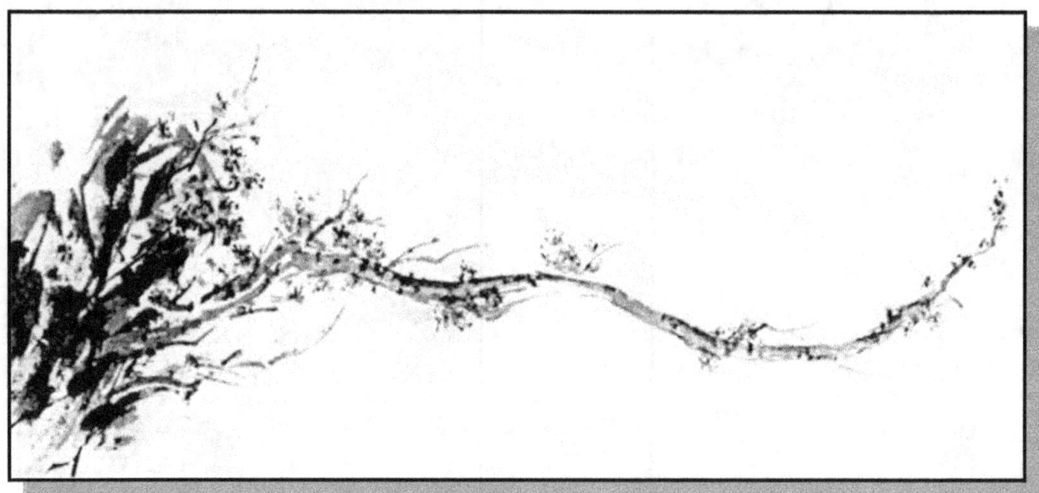

How to Stretch and
Wet-Mount a Sumi-e Painting

Glue:

There are many acid-free glues available that can be used for this purpose.I give instructions to make your own from the gluten in organic flour. Non-organic flour will contain pesticide residue and thus will not be appropriate.

Nori Paste from Yasutomo is an excellent choice - thin with distilled water and keep refrigerated.

Supplies:
1. Your painting.
2. A piece of washi — possibly a bit heavier than your painting depending upon the paper used — cut 2" larger than your painting.
3. Wide soft brush for spreading the glue.
4. Wide brush to use for smoothing out wrinkles, etc.
5. Mister bottle filled with water, preferably non-chlorinated.
6. Glue as described above.
7. A large straw such as the kind provided when you purchase a smoothie, although thinner straws will also work. The straw can be re-used.
8. A wooden or laminated board large enough to accommodate your pictures. You can use both sides of the board.
9. A small brush to spread a thin line of glue.
10. A thin knife or exacto.
11. Spectrafix — see spectrafix.com or your local art supplier. It is a non-toxic alternative to many other workable fixatives.

Method:

1. If your painting has watercolour on it, first spray with Spectrafix, both sides, to help prevent the colours smudging.
2. Place your painting and the cut washi on your table, both good side down.
3. Place a strip of plain washi under one corner of your painting that will hang past the edges of the top sheet of washi, to make it easier to lift the work after gluing.
4. If you have used a fair bit of watercolour in your painting, or the paper is very fragile when wet, place a plain piece of dampened and smoothed inexpensive washi beneath the good side of your painting. It will absorb any colour that may spread during mounting and hold the paper together, if fragile. If you have used colour in just a few places, used bits of dampened flattened washi beneath those areas.
5. Spray all of them with a fine spray of water to dampen your painting and flatten it, before gluing, with a clean dry brush.
6. Spray the washi you will be mounting on with water as well.
7. Dampen your glue brush and carefully spread glue on your painting, brushing from the middle outward, eliminating air bubbles and creasing. It is best if your painting is fairly wet, but not so wet that it will tear easily, as the glue will wet it even more!
8. Lift the larger sheet of paper onto your painting, leaving the 2" border all around, and gently brush it smooth from centre to edges with the dry brush.
9. Carefully lift one corner of the larger paper. If the painting has not adhered, just lift the corner of the painting and hold it onto the top paper and then lift the entirety off the table and place it down again where the larger paper used to be.
10. Run a thin bead of glue all around the outer edge with the small brush.
11. Lift the painting onto the board — the side edged with glue touching the board — and brush it smooth using your dry brush, ensuring the edges have adhered to the board.
12. Lift one corner of the painting and insert the straw.
13. Blow gently to lift the painting from the board — you can see this happening.
14. Remove the straw and re-press the corner onto the board.
15. Leave the painting to dry thoroughly. This may take several hours or overnight.
16. Thoroughly wash the glue out of your brushes.
17. To remove the stretched painting, you can cut it off within the edges of glue with the exacto (preferred manner), or you can gently lift one edge and insert the thin knife and run it around the painting, lifting the edges off the board.
18. Use water and a cloth to clean your board.

How to Mount Onto a Wood Frame – Birch Plywood Panel

Tools:

1. Wood frame.
2. Washi a little larger than wood frame.
3. TriArt UV Protective Medium Semi-gloss, any clear acrylic medium, gesso or titanium buff which will even out the substrate colour and alkalize the surface.
4. Your painting - preferably with slightly larger than the finished piece will be.
5. Acid-free glue.
6. 2" to 3" hake brush for spreading glue, and another 2" to 3" hake brush to spread acrylic medium.
7. Wide brush to use for smoothing out wrinkles, etc.
8. Spray bottle filled with water, preferably non-chlorinated.
9. Wood block with fine sandpaper attached.
10. SpectraFix spray or other fixative of your choice.

Method:

1. Ensure the surface of the wood frame is clean and dry.
2. Lay your painting on the wood frame where you would like it to sit. Gently fold down the edges to make a slight impression. Cut off any large excess of paper on the painting but leave at least ¼" edge if possible.
3. If your painting has watercolour on it, spray it lightly on both sides with SpectraFix spray to set it and follow the instructions above for mounting a painting where watercolour has been used (step 4 above). Spectrafix is also used on papers that tend to pill.
4. Paint a thin layer of acrylic medium, or titanium buff on the frame to alkalize the surface.
5. Mount the painting onto another piece of washi as described in steps 2 through 6 of "How to Stretch and Wet-Mount a Sumi-e Painting."
6. While the mounted painting is still wet, spread glue on either the plain sheet of paper you have just attached to your painting (this is the preferred method, but not as feasible with really large pieces) or onto the wood block. Settle the painting where you want it on the wood block and smooth from centre to edges with your dry brush.

7.   When the paper is dry, use a wood block with fine sandpaper to remove excess paper around the edge of the wood frame

8.   Spread two thin layers of semi-gloss acrylic medium over the finished mounted painting, following the direction of the picture with your brushstrokes, allowing it to dry between coats.

9.   The finished work can be framed in a float frame or left unframed.

Making your own acid-free glue:

1.   In a small container, place a small amount of organic flour, about ½ cup, and mix it with about three times as much water until no lumps remain. Cover and place in the fridge for three or four days.

2.   Remove from the fridge and pour off any liquid that has accumulated. Reach in and pull out the gooey elastic substance that is left, and place it in a small saucepan.

3.   Add about twice as much water and mix thoroughly. Place on low to medium heat and stir continuously until small bubbles form. DO NOT LET IT BOIL!

4.   Remove from heat and place in a container to cool. At this point you can add one or two drops of grapefruit seed extract to inhibit mould. The mixture will thicken and become rather solid.

5.   Store the glue in the fridge.

6.   Before using, take a small amount of this solid glue and mix with water until it is the consistency of thin pudding. Push it through a sieve to remove all lumps.

Composition

You have very little to create a dynamic composition — texture, depth of the shades of gray/black, yohaku (white space), and your hanko (name stamp) with its splash of red.

When producing your painting, consider the balance of triangular shapes for the painted areas and those that are not painted.

Painted and unpainted areas should create asymmetry in the work.

Also important are variations in shading and texture.

If one area is painted in light ink, another can be darker.

If one area is painted with a dry brush, paint another with a wetter brush.

If you are pleased with your painting, your final consideration is the placement of the hanko.

Placement should appear "modest," as the spot of red complements the rest of the painting. It is your signature, not the prime area.

The hanko is also the place the viewer's eye will go to first, after which it will travel through the painting.

Have your hanko on a slip of rice paper to try it in several spots.

See what part of the painting is emphasized by different placements.

If you have carved several stamps, consider the size and shape of the stamp with relation to the painting, as well as its meaning.

Over all, your painting must appear natural and spontaneous.

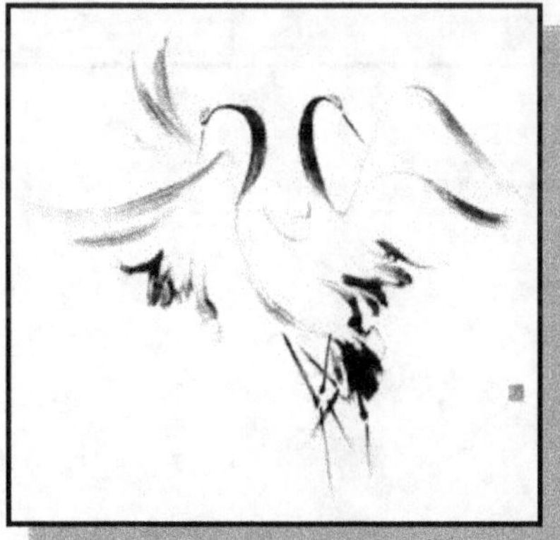

**Courtship Dance by the author
Hanko is "Water"**

What Next?

Next is practice, practice and more practice.

Choose a subject you like to paint and try it in many ways, always simplifying.

Paint it as you wish and then try leaving out one brushstroke. If that works, leave out another, continuing until you have a recognizable subject with as few brushstrokes as possible. If it does not work, try to leave out a different brushstroke.

Eventually you will see things in the form of brushstrokes. The world will change before your eyes and your brush will capture all you see.

Recognize forms and subjects that appeal to your artistic soul and paint them to continue to grow on this incredible journey — always moving Body, Breath and Brush together to focus body and spirit onto the end of your brush.

Even if sumi-e is not really how you want to paint, by following this book you will have learned a new way to use a brush that includes the whole of your body and spirit. You can apply what you have learned to whatever art form you choose.

You will be able to dance with brush, pencil, pastels or in whatever your chosen medium may be.

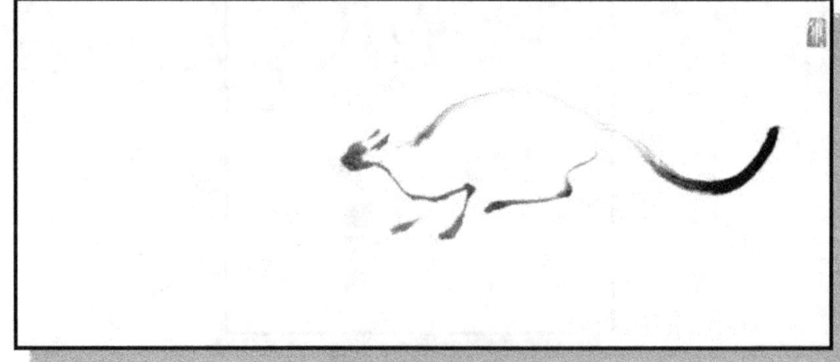

"On the Fly" by the author
Hanko is 'Elegant'

About the Author

Roslyn Levin's earliest memories of painting are from the age of three, when she used watercolours to paint frogs found in the family's flooded basement after Hurricane Hazel passed through Toronto.

She always wanted to be a professional artist, but was side-tracked until 1981, when she gave up her career as a Computer Systems Analyst with the Canadian Government in Ottawa to pursue her dream.

Her success in her first solo exhibit in 1982 at Ottawa's then Braam Gallery encouraged her to continue, with successful annual solo exhibits over the following years.

She began teaching sumi-e at the Guelph School of Art in 1998 and has enjoyed sharing her love of sumi-e with hundreds of students since then in Guelph, Orangeville, Barrie, and throughout Toronto. She has even had students travel to her studio from the US to learn her technique.

At the time of this printing, Ms. Levin has been the recipient of many awards, including three Ruth Yamada Awards for excellence in sumi-e from Sumi-e Artists of Canada, and nine first prizes for her shodo (Japanese calligraphy) from Japanese juries through Shodo Canada.

Ms. Levin is an elected member of Sumi-e Artists of Canada, where she serves as Membership Chair, and the Society of Canadian Artists.

Ms. Levin is also a founding member and Secretary of Brushfire Artists in Orangeville, Ontario.

Ms. Levin lives in Shelburne, Ontario, with her husband, Andrew Cherry, and her cat/model, Sweetie.

For more than 20 years, her studio has been in Dragonfly Arts on Broadway, in Orangeville, Ontario.

She loves visitors, so contact her to come and show her what you have painted after following instructions in this book!

Her website is www.artbyroslyn.on.ca

Supplies
The Japanese Paper Place   www.japanesepaperplace.com
103 The East Mall #1, Etobicoke, ON M8Z 5X9 CANADA

Hirao Bunmeido   www.hireobunmeido.com
5-7-24 Jonohori Kumano-chou Aki-gun Hiroshima 731-4215 Japan

Awagami Factory   www.awagami.or.jp
136 Kawahigashi, Yamakawa-cho, Yoshinogawa-shi, Tokushima, Japan 779-3401

Shoyu   www.shoyu- net.jp
Shoyu Nara (main store), Osaka, Kyoto and online stores

Ichi Inc.   www.worlds-oldest-inksticks.jp 4-6-16,
Anryu, Suminoe-ku, Osaka 559-0003, Japan

Osaka Kyoikush   www.osakakyouzai.com
Japanese Calligraphy Supplies

Shih Tai Arts and Crafts   www.shihtaiarts.com
290 Yorktech Dr Unit#21, Markham, ON L6G 0A7 CANADA

................many other places may be found online or perhaps where you live.

www.ingramcontent.com/pod-product-compliance
Lightning Source LLC
Chambersburg PA
CBHW080341030726
47595CB00012B/4089